You Hold Us While We Grow

You Hold Us While We Grow

Tim Cook

Foreword by Barbara Cook

Transcribed and Edited by
Peter and Christina Haas

Published by
ContemplativeChristians.com

2900 W. Anderson Lane C-200-117
Austin, TX 78757

You Hold Us While We Grow
Copyright © 2011 by Tim Cook.
Introduction Copyright
© 2011 by Peter Traben Haas.
All Rights Reserved.

Published 2011.
Printed in the United States of America.

ISBN-13 978-0-615-48488-4

Library of Congress Cataloging-in-Publication Data

Cook, Tim
You Hold Us While We Grow: Selected Sermons and Prayers
1. Spirituality – Christianity. 2. Sermons. I. Title
BV.4501.C39 2011

Cover design by Travis Hardy Design. Austin, TX.

Image of Tim Cook courtesy of Randall Ford Studio, Austin, TX. ©2011.
All Rights Reserved.

The Publisher wishes to express special gratitude to Dan McGowan
Consulting, Mary Anne Best and Ken Ely for their review and improve-
ments to the text, and to Vivek Bakshi for his generous production support and funding.

∞

*ContemplativeChristians.com is an online resource for the contemplative
Christian journey into the love of God.*

Dedicated to

Our Teachers

&

The contemplative Christian community at

The Church of Conscious Harmony

Contents

∞

"I have said these things to you so that my joy may be in you, and that your joy may be complete."

-   *John 15.11*

"This Work, if you will listen to it and hear it in your hearts, is the most beautiful thing you could possibly hear. It speaks not of sin, but of being asleep..."

-   Maurice Nicoll, *Psychological Commentaries, Page 10*

"In fact, the Hermit...haunts the imagination of [spiritual seekers], the Hermit of legend and the Hermit of history was, is, and always will be the solitary man with the lamp, mantle and staff. For he possesses the gift of letting light shine in the darkness – this is his "lamp"; he has the faculty of separating himself from the collective moods, prejudices and desires of race, nation, class and family – the faculty of reducing to silence the cacophony of collectivism vociferating around him, in order to listen to and understand the hierarchical harmony of the spheres – this is his "mantle"; at the same time he possesses a sense of realism which is so developed that he stands in the domain of reality not on two feet, but rather on three, i.e. he advances only after having *touched* the ground through immediate experience and at first-hand contact without intermediaries – this is his 'staff.'"

-   *Letter IX, The Hermit* from
    Meditations on the Tarot

Foreword

By Barbara Cook

∞

When I met Tim in Boulder, Colorado in 1980, he was already well on his spiritual journey. We met at work and began spending quite a bit of time talking together there. He had just returned from a pilgrimage to India and was still aglow. Tim shared with me the complete story of his Indian journey, an amazing pilgrimage whose details I can still recall.

I found myself surprisingly drawn to his vivid retelling even though I was agnostic, having left the church some 15 years before. It was at that time Tim told me he was going to apply to be a minister. I remember thinking that was interesting, but that it really had nothing to do with me.

After Tim left our common place of employment, he came back to pick up his last paycheck, timing it when he knew I would be there. It was then that he asked me out on our first date. We went on a long motorcycle ride through the beautiful Flatiron Mountains surrounding Boulder with another couple we knew from work. After our ride we sat in conversation with the young couple, and Tim started talking about God. Although this was a realm that I had been fairly out of touch with, everything he said seemed to be true, to make sense. It seemed so for the other young man in our group too. I remember him saying, "Tim, I know you are right, I just cannot know this yet!"

Later, as we were going home, Tim said to me, "You know Barbara, you are an existentialist." I was familiar with the term and thought I knew what it meant, but not in relationship to myself. So I asked, "What exactly do you mean?" and Tim said, "You believe that God just wound all of this existence up at the beginning, and is letting everybody figure out for themselves how best to be in it." I responded, "Yes, I think that sounds right." Then, just for fun, he brought up the name of an intellectual Buddhist we had worked with and said, "You are just like him!" For the first time I could see myself from the outside.

I asked Tim, "So what do you believe about God?" He said, "I do not *believe* anything!" With that declaration, Tim continued to share his story, "I was at a point in my life when everything was falling apart. I had lost my job; I was in debt over my head; my ex-wife and her boyfriend had taken the bed and my stereo. Desperate, I fell down to my knees and cried out, 'I cannot take this anymore!' Suddenly, a wave of peace descended on me. I felt how I always wanted to feel: loved and held. I knew things before words, and I felt I could have stayed in that amazing place, that somehow I had graduated. But then I remembered my three Old English Sheepdogs and thought, I have got to get back to care for my dogs! Still, from then on things were different. I knew I was part of a very *present whole*. Wholeness is love, healing and returning things to order. Everything in my world began changing, including relationships, which began to be more loving."

"So," Tim concluded, "I do not believe anything. It is an *experience* of the presence of God, and I can never *not* know that, whatever the appearances."

I sat up all night pondering our conversation. Yes, during childhood I had learned in church that God was love, but I could not say I remembered having experienced that Love personally. Still, what Tim spoke of was very evocative of my early church teaching. I then remembered a time when my parents had first started going to church. There *was* love all around, a tangible substance. My dad started reading us *The Greatest Story Ever Told*, a retelling of the Bible. There was God and there was Love!

Reflecting further, I found that during the past 15 years of my life, after I had gained intellectual sophistication in college and parted ways with the church, I did not seem to know anybody who went to church, or who even talked about God. But then a few names began coming back to me. I recalled those I knew who went to church, a few friends and some relatives, but not that many people. Still, of those I recalled, there were some very good people. I pondered, "did God/Love do that to people?"

The next morning when I woke I had my own personal experience with that Presence and I knew. Even more, I *knew* that I knew, and that this was to be what my life would be about: knowing God! I could see clearly why nothing had worked out in my life or to my satisfaction so far. I had not yet been on my purpose to know God, love God and serve God! But from that day on, I have been on the spiritual journey with my life partner, Tim.

As a young man Tim had been quite depressed. His college counselor at Boston University told him he was the most depressed person she had ever tested. From Boston, Tim transferred to CU Boulder where he graduated, secure in his confirmation of depression. Soon after college he was declared 4-F (unsuitable to serve in the U.S. Armed Forces) and moved directly to Canada.

With the explosion of change that occurred during the 1960's - cities being burned, assassinations, and protests - Tim could not understand what was happening in Vietnam or America. While in Toronto, one of his coworkers gave him the book, *The Wisdom of Insecurity* by Alan Watts.

He told Tim, "You look like the kind of guy who could understand this stuff. But I warn you, once you start thinking about it, you will never be able to stop!" Tim thought to himself, "I can think or not think anything I want to!" Amazingly, reading that slim book back in 1969 began to change Tim's life forever. From that point on, Tim looked high and low in probably every possible quarter for this elusive God, this new conscious understanding and way of being.

By the time I met Tim, he had been meditating for some time and had already discovered many paths that were still not *the* path. While he was seeking, Tim observed within himself that he would remember and forget, remember and forget this awareness, but still longed to know God all the time. In fact, during that time, Tim would get up very early, without waking or telling me, just to pray and do his spiritual practice. Even in those first years of our relationship, his time with God was his priority. Later, he would have the courage to tell me about this daily practice, and soon we began waking and praying together.

I recall that a cousin of Tim's was passing through and told him that he went to a church where they meditated, believed in the universality of God, and that it was also a Christian church! So, Tim went to see for himself. As he walked through the doors of the Unity Church in Denver, Colorado, he heard a clear, interior voice say, "I am going to be a Unity minister." He thought this a somewhat strange idea at the time, but realized that this would truly be the one way that he could remember God, and be immersed in God.

Shortly after Tim and I started dating, he applied and was accepted to the Unity Ministerial School. When asked why he wanted to become a Unity minister, he told his board, "I want to be immersed in God, and I think this is a good way to do it." I thought that was an honest response, but shouldn't he be saying, I want to help people, or save souls or whatever? But being honest always serves. Growth is almost always accompanied by some discomfort (like any good birthing), and although I worked in the Unity prayer room, praying for others for hours a day, and Tim was immersed in God through deep study and contemplation, we went through what we now tenderly call "The Great Holy Wars." Tim and I began to learn what love really meant, and how to be humans in God together. Looking back now, I will say that it was our willingness to trust God, in spite of appearances, and our dedication to continuing our daily spiritual practices, "Holy Wars" or not, that transformed our relationship.

Our first church placement was the answer to our heartfelt prayer to go where we could serve, be served and grow in Christ. We loved Boulder and our little church community there, but they already had a wonderful minister who also loved Boulder, so we knew we would be headed out of our beloved Colorado. Each day when we prayed to go where God would have us go, we would throw in, "God, our church could be in a ghetto in New York City, or a small farm town in Iowa," we did not believe we wanted to go to either, but we were willing. Still, when Austin, Texas came into our awareness, it took 13 phone calls from Ritchie Mintz, our dear friend from Boulder who had moved to Austin to get us to even send our resume to the church there.

I guess being from the mountains of Colorado, Texas was not on our radar. Tim went down to Austin to give the little church a trial sermon. After his talk he called me and said, "This is our church! This is our town!" And it was. Our four years in that precious church in the Oaks were amazing. We went from perhaps a couple of hundred people to 900 people attending three Sunday services, up to 250 students attending Wednesday night classes, and 50 to 90 new members joining quarterly. It was quite an experience. Throughout all the excitement and numerical growth during our time at Unity, Tim continued studying and searching for more of God.

Eventually we felt a call of a different kind and left that church, staying out of ministry for a year. We joined a non-Christian, higher consciousness community, a place where we thought we could grow spiritually. But at the end of that year, Tim knew emphatically that he was Christian, and so that was that. We left.

We went back into a small ministry in Kansas City to reflect about where we were and what we needed to do.
After that year we felt we would continue in ministry and
continue our deepening search for God. Yet, we ques-
tioned if we could simply take a job as ministers within a
church where, although people thought the spiritual
journey was interesting, they were not particularly devoted to transformation in Christ. We desired much more
than merely church on Sundays. We wondered, "Could
Christians make God the center of their lives?" In our
travels we had seen many Buddhist communities and ash-
rams, several of them with Western practitioners. But
could Western Christians be devoted practitioners? A
mentor suggested we go back to Austin where we had a
group of spiritual friends, and where Tim had been returning monthly to teach a class on the Work (psychological transformation as presented by Maurice Nicoll). Tim
asked the 24 people in his class if they would be interested in a five-year experiment in Christian esoteric community.

The community would be a community of daily practice
requiring: rising at 5 a.m. for daily meditation, daily study
of spiritual works, two Work groups a week, service to the
church community, tithing and Sunday worship. It was a
stringent list of requirements to set forth, and we wondered if people would be willing to commit, but Tim
knew that he wanted to be with people who were really
interested in being transformed in Christ. Besides, we
were just asking for people to do what we were committed to throughout our journey together.

That was in July of 1988. The five-year experiment began
in our living room. It was the beginning of The Church of

Conscious Harmony (CCH) and the Tenth Man School. Over the years I have observed Tim having a profound effect on people's relationship with God. Some, like myself, began their journey back toward Reality. Others, Tim has helped to deepen their God-experience. I think it has always been Tim's hunger for a deeper experience of God, along with his truthfulness and humility, which have helped others trust God on their spiritual journey.

It all seems to have been ordained, one event unfolding from another at the perfect time. We were a few months into this experiment when a spiritual friend, Jewish psychiatrist Carl Kirsch, gave Tim a book on Christian contemplative life and practices, *Open Mind, Open Heart,* written by a Cistercian monk, Father Thomas Keating. I have always known Tim to voraciously read books on spiritual transformation. He has devoured books on higher Hindu and Buddhist teachings, often reading aloud with me. This book was no different, but it would change everything for us.

Tim and I had also both been initiated into meditation by an Indian teacher, the late Nityananda, and practiced daily for years. Then here, all of the sudden, this simple, concise book gave us an understanding of Christianity we had totally missed! In Centering Prayer we now had the missing piece and knew we were home. Tim contacted Father Keating who graciously agreed to teach Centering Prayer to the Tenth Man School and CCH. So began our long and blessed relationship with Father Thomas.

When Tim eventually drew up the incorporation papers for the church, he did so stating that the church was for the sole purpose of assisting those on the journey of transformation into Christ. It states that there are two legs of the church, Centering Prayer from the Christian monastic contemplative tradition, and the inner work of Christianity from the Orthodox monastic tradition.

Students in the Tenth Man School agree and desire to a commitment of making God the center of their lives, utilizing the two legs upon which the church stands. Those who attend the church are invited to participate in, but not required to have a daily practice. Our participation with Centering Prayer, which happened in the first three months of our experiment, gave the church its full name: The Church of Conscious Harmony ~ A Contemplative Christian Fellowship.

After the first five years we unanimously decided to continue for five more. Presently, in the year 2011, there are 60 committed members in the Tenth Man School for Christian transformation, and approximately 250 members in the church. We have moved onto our own campus located on twelve acres of beautiful Texas Hill Country where we have a sanctuary, meditation chapel, spacious youth classrooms, offices, library and bookstore. We have a thriving youth ministry based on Godly Play and *Lectio Divina*, loved by the adult leaders and young people alike.

Our affiliation throughout all this time with Contemplative Outreach, Ltd. (a network of people and groups practicing Centering Prayer worldwide founded by Father Thomas Keating), which exists as a way of connecting with others who are opening to God through silence and scripture. Father Thomas founded it as a means of information, formation and support on the spiritual journey. Through this affiliation, we sponsor many Centering

Prayer retreats each year. CCH also sponsors a weekly Centering Prayer and Emotions Anonymous support group at Hobby Prison for Women in Marlin, Texas. We offer Introduction to Centering Prayer workshops, teaching hundreds of people this simple yet transformative relationship to God.

This experiment was the result of divine guidance from within and from without, and is the fruit of our simple faith to listen and follow God's leading. Any good that has resulted is the work of the Holy Spirit and our willingness to consent. CCH leadership has also expanded beyond Tim and me. Each member of the CCH board of directors has been practicing both the Work and Centering Prayer for years. The board receives Communion together, prays in silence before each monthly meeting and ends each meeting with intercessory prayer. Everyone who has responded to the call, and who has taken up the daily practice has grown in grace and stature through Christ. We have all witnessed miracles of love and grace. We have consented to God's presence and action in our lives. We have grown. Our community has grown. How good and gracious is our God.

At this time I see we are part of the wider community of Christians who are seeking an experience of Christ rather than just knowing about Christ. In his book, *Falling Upward*, Father Richard Rohr has called this stage of the spiritual journey the second stage of life. I feel our CCH experiment has proven that anyone seeking the deeper or contemplative dimension of the gospel can receive it with a daily relationship with God through Centering Prayer and a way to participate in the dismantling of our false self system, for which we have used the Work of interior

Christianity. We have experienced that God wants us to bloom in Christ and will support even our meager efforts.

When we began this experiment we called ourselves a monastery without walls, a place devoted to getting into orbit around God without leaving the world. We have heeded Father Thomas' invitation "to become ordinary people living out of God's extraordinary love." I believe this experiment has revealed that everyone is qualified and is called. I also believe every church has all it needs, if it just adds the living water of Centering Prayer and the desire to take Jesus the Christ up on his revelation of who we humans are and can be. The Church of Conscious Harmony is a living witness that one can still be in the world while on the transformational journey, without needing to be sealed off in a physical monastery.

Since Tim and I met in Boulder, Colorado in 1980, our marriage and our life have been centered on the spiritual journey, the journey of movement from the head to the heart. Over the years, we have continued to grow deeper and richer in our experience of Christ and for one another. That includes the healing of our childhood wounds, the unloading of the emotional debris of a lifetime, and discovering who we are and who God is. It has at once been difficult, tedious, heart wrenching, and also simple, joy-filled and totally rewarding.

As Bernadette Roberts, a Christian Mystic and friend, has said, "In the journey toward God, though it appears often difficult or impossible, in reality, you will not even stub your little toe." Or, as Father Thomas has said, "Once you have said 'yes' to God, then everything is working for your healing and union with God – if you say yes to it!" This has been our experience, though at times we have been slow at saying yes. So, I bring this foreword to a close with deep gratitude to all those who have journeyed with us at The Church of Conscious Harmony and to those God has placed in our lives as mentors along the way. May Christ continue to be victorious.

I also give special thanks to our friend Peter Haas, who has found particular inspiration and insight on the spiritual journey through Tim and the community here at The Church of Conscious Harmony. With dedication and labors Peter, with the help of his wife and spiritual partner Christina, has put together this collection of Tim's messages in book form.

Personally, over the past 29 years of listening to Tim teach multiple times a week, his sermons still call, feed, remind and inspire me on my own ongoing journey, and I pray that this book may be an encouragement and of great use to others embarking on this journey, those who long to move from the point of merely knowing about God to making God the center of their lives and ministries. May it be so.

Introduction:

Sermons that bring Christ close

By Peter Traben Haas

∞

T he following collection of sermons and prayers is presented in printed form for those who value Tim's preaching and teaching. Our wish is that wider distribution of these sermons will be useful for the continued unfolding of contemplative Christianity in our time.

The collection you now hold in your hands is comprised of a sampling of sermons and prayers shared by Pastor Tim Cook at The Church of Conscious Harmony (CCH) in Austin, Texas from 2009 to 2010. I trust you will find them to be just as edifying and useful for your spiritual journey as you would sitting in the CCH sanctuary at the time of their first giving. And if you were there in person, I wish their printed form to revivify your heart and mind with the remembrance of your own growth through the unique and important teaching that comes through as Tim speaks.

Since Tim's preaching style is quite fluid, listening to him can often feel like drinking from a fire hose; this presents challenges to transcribers. Thus, in this collection, we have taken what we hope is an appropriate liberty in editing Tim's spoken word, showcasing the flow and poetry of his logic and language, while removing miscellaneous filler, transitions and quotations that do not translate well from spoken to written word. If we have misrepresented Tim in any way to you in our editing process, please forgive these shortcomings; they are ours, not Tim's.

While I would love to include more of Tim's sermons, time, space and practicality dictate otherwise. In Part One, the process of selection was primarily based on sermons that were personally meaningful to me and that seemed to represent some of the core theological themes undergirding Tim's preaching. The sermons in Part Two required less sorting, since the intention was to convey the Christian liturgical year, and as such, the sermons were more easily identified. The prayers were selected after reviewing all of the recorded services during 2009 and 2010. I trust it represents a sampling of Tim's pastoral prayers that help us remember ourselves and worship God. While reading a sermon is not the same as hearing it in person, I sense Tim's written words still resonate with the warmth and love conveyed in the tone of his voice and physical presence.

The aim to collect, transcribe, edit and produce this collection of sermons began during the Taizé New Year's Eve worship service at CCH in 2009. During the part of the service where participants are invited to kneel at the cross, I felt led to do this project as a personal gift to Tim, pastor to Pastor. In the spirit of full disclosure, I serve a neighboring church and have had the privilege of getting to know Tim as a friend and colleague. His counsel, friendship and teaching have deeply blessed and formed me. It is also important to acknowledge that this project is not an official publication of CCH. The sermons and prayers are intended to be a spiritual resource for Christians seeking a different kind of Christianity. I trust it will also be a tangible celebration of Tim's ongoing pastoral ministry.

While this introduction and following collection of sermons does not intend to provide a general survey of CCH, or of Tim's theological formation and philosophy of ministry, such a work would be a useful study serving the further flourishing of the contemplative Christian dimension. What can be said definitively here is that what began as a five year experiment in Christian community has resplendently taken flight by the Spirit, while simultaneously taking root in silence and sacrament. Indeed, through sermon, prayer and Eucharist, in and among this extraordinary yet common congregation of spiritual friends, people are awaking to the truth of their Real Being in Christ. The remainder of this introduction intends to situate Tim's teaching and the elements of worship at CCH within the Christian theological tradition. If this is not of interest, please skip these pages and delve into Tim's sermons.

Having been personally blessed by Tim Cook's teaching and preaching over the last several years, I have come to the conclusion that the value of Tim's teaching and preaching is of historic significance. Here is one reason why. As a teacher, Tim uniquely gathers several strands of the Christian tradition, and in so doing revives an ancient approach to the interpretation of the Christian scriptures for the purpose of personal transformation into Christ. As such, Tim stands within the tradition that is best summarized as "inner Christianity," or "esoteric Christianity," or to some, the "Christian hermetic tradition," which all rely heavily upon the allegorical or "depth" reading of the scriptures.

Yet, Tim also brings several other dimensions to the table – I should say, *chair* – such as: integrating evolutionary and developmental ideas with Christian presuppositions; harmonizing interreligious views with key Christian doctrines; an integrated view of human suffering; the spiritual purpose of the liturgical year, and putting the contemplative Christian tradition in conversation with the teaching of G.I. Gurdjieff as interpreted especially through the *Psychological Commentaries* of Maurice Nicoll. Possibly most important of all is the central unifying and sapiential function of the Eucharist for the spiritual journey and life in community.

These are a few of the dimensions of Tim's unique contribution to contemplative Christianity, but none are so beloved as his vulnerable sharing of personal life stories and illuminative, heart-opening examples. I am certain many listeners have their favorites – like his rough and tough rugby days; his love of motorcycles and the Packers; his conversion in the Unity church in Boulder, Colorado; his early letters to Bernadette Roberts; his stays with Father Thomas Keating; travels in India, and of course his adventures in marriage(s)! Undoubtedly, Tim would be uncomfortable with this claim to historical importance within the contemplative Christian tradition. However, in time, I believe it will become evident just how unique a role Tim has played in the post-modern era of Christianity. Here are two reasons why:

First, CCH rests upon the union of two foundations hitherto (as far as I know) never combined in a church: *Centering Prayer*, as popularized by Thomas Keating, and *The Work*, as articulated by Maurice Nicoll. The union of these two dimensions of Christianity, in the form of a non-denominational church has created a new expression of Christian community within the spectrum of Christian history.

Second, at a time of increasing cultural fragmentation, with fears rising at a global scale, many church leaders are looking for effective models that foster personal transformation and nurture authentic community. While Christian leaders have tended to appreciate the contemplative model for their personal formation, applying such contemplative insights into their church communities has often proven more challenging, perhaps because there are so few living examples of contemplative churches available. Thus, as a living contemplative community, CCH can provide just such a model.

Tim and Barbara's visionary work in co-creating a model of contemplative Christian community dedicated to personal and corporate transformation in Christ, gathering for the sole purpose of God-devotion as a monastery without walls and so refining the process of dying to self and living to God (Galatians 2.20), indicates that CCH is a very positive developmental occurrence in the ongoing unfolding of Christianity in our time.

∞

In an effort to paint a picture of the uniqueness of a few dimensions of the worship experience at CCH and their connection with the Christian tradition, let us turn our attention to the sanctuary in which these sermons were given, and to a few of my personal observations while worshiping at CCH.

Sermons at The Church of Conscious Harmony are shared from the seated position in a comfortable looking chair placed in the center of a platform about three feet above the congregation, and ten feet from the front row. Directly above the chair is a large, suspended wooden cross, beams lashed together, hanging beneath the octagon windowed cupola approximately thirty feet above. Out of sight, directly beneath the sanctuary floor is the Theosis Chapel, a thirty-seat space ideal for Centering Prayer. The Theosis chapel literally and silently undergirds everything that occurs in the sanctuary. The platform upon which the chair sits is encircled by eight clusters of support beams that extend up into the octagon cupola, creating a tepee-like feel for the sanctuary ceiling.

Directly above the teacher's chair in the CCH sanctuary is an octagonal, windowed cupola. Above the cupola, crowning the church stands a cross. Beneath the cupola, a wooden beam descends a quarter of the way down from the windows toward the platform in the sanctuary. It seems to represent the descent of Truth, encircled by the octagon. The octagon shares similarities to other images within the Work teaching, such as the Enneagram symbol, as well as the Mark, which is also the logo for the CCH community. The CCH logo represents our True Life within the Trinity, encircled by the movement of the Spirit. Please notice the similarities and distinctions of the images – the Octagon, the Enneagram and the Mark:

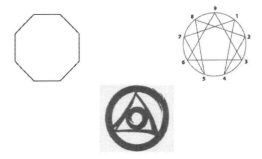

Having reflected upon these aforementioned "architec-tural" details and having personally felt the influences of the CCH worship space and symbols, it seems that the sanctuary design conveys essential information about the intentions and foundations of this unique Christian community. For example, while many preachers stand lecture style to deliver their sermons, the seated position more visibly conveys the integration of the vertical and the horizontal. From a side profile, the seated teacher appears in simplified form as such:

|—

This leads us to ask the question "What might the im-portance of the teacher's seated position be in relation-ship to the Christian tradition and pastoral ministry?" One answer is that the seated position is an adaptation of the traditional posture of the sage, sitting upright, legs crossed in prayer or meditation. The seated position is integrated symbolically in that the vertical inspiration of truth and wisdom connects into the horizontal world of experience and relationships within the physical embodiment of the teacher. In the realm of Christian teaching, the seated position is an intimation of the complete symbol of the cross, which represents the full embodiment of the vertical and horizontal, otherwise known in the Christian tradition as *the Incarnation*, that is, the union of the human and the divine in the person Jesus of Nazareth. The "cross" appears in simplified form, completing the seated position multi-dimensionally as thus:

Since the cross is the inexhaustible symbol of the breadth, length, height and depth of the love of Christ (Ephesians 3.18-19), the presence and action of divine love symbolized by the cross continues in the present through the ministry of the Word, often referred to simply as "preaching" or "teaching." This ministry of the Word is the continuation of one office within the nested hierarchy of the Christian church – namely the pastor/teacher office referred to variously in Scripture as bishop *(episcopos)* or elder *(presbyteros)*, both words conveying the idea of "overseer."

In this way, the Incarnation continues through the preached word of those who have come under the authority of the cross, and the one who occupied it, the Lord Jesus Christ. Thus, pastors are servants and ambassadors of Jesus Christ, remaining at their post, virtually immobilized by the weight of their "crown" of calling and rooted to their "throne" of responsibility from which they sit, listen and speak. The office of pastor and teacher is one of listening and receiving grace so to serve in love under the authority of Jesus Christ. Pastors are, in the best sense, under orders from on high, partaking in the ongoing mission of divine love as articulated in the apostolic formula and final charge of Jesus:

> *"All authority in heaven and on earth has been given to me. Go therefore and make disciples of all nations, baptizing them in the name of the Father, and of the Son and of the Holy Spirit, and teaching them to obey everything I have commanded you. And remember, I am with you always, to the end of the age"* (Matthew 28.18-20).

The anointing of the Spirit that initiates this ongoing ministry of the Word in an individual follows the template of Jesus' baptism (Matthew 3) and the event of Pentecost (Acts 3), both empowering preaching and spiritual healing, first in the person of Jesus and second in the person of Peter. In both cases, but to varying degrees, it is important to note that while the power of the Spirit anointed both for extraordinary ministry, the Spirit also led them into immediate personal suffering. In the case of Jesus, it was forty days in the wilderness, praying and fasting and dealing with intense spiritual temptations (Matthew 4), and in Peter's case, imprisonment (Acts 5). All this is to say, the way of the anointed pastor is often one of suffering. Such suffering of an anointed one tempers the common temptation toward grandiosity associated with the very public role of the teacher.

In summary, perhaps the above architectural details and liturgical symbols in the CCH sanctuary and community convey that the teacher ministers in the chair under the authority of the Christian Tradition (symbolized by the cross), as well as the authority of the Work teachings (symbolized by the octagon/Enneagram shape); vertically connected with Truth coming from above (symbolized by the lone descending beam), encircled by the eight pillars of Wisdom, which are, perhaps, the lived experience recorded in the sacred writings and experiences of the human wisdom traditions from every direction of the planet from which the Spirit blows: east, west, north and south. Thus, the inspiration of the Holy Spirit integrates the vertical dimension of prophetic truth, with the horizontal dimension of lived experience under the authority of Jesus Christ symbolized at CCH by a simple chair underneath a common, rough-hewn cross.

Since this is a collection of sermons and prayers, it might be useful to say something about the preacher's voice and physical presence. In my experience, the feeling of Tim's vocal intonation and presence is loving kindness. Resonant, warm and compassionate, Tim's smile and voice speak volumes without ever having to say a word. It is no surprise then that Tim views CCH as the church of St. John, in contrast to the church of St. Peter. Remember, it was the beloved disciple John who rested upon the Lord's heart. That is, St. John experienced the love of God in Jesus relationally, not rationally. This relational experience of love plays out on Sunday mornings in many ways, but one in particular is through a common song of response, "The gospel in one word is love," sung in a round to a simple tune. Nurturing the love of God and love of one another is, from my perspective, a chief feature of Tim's preaching and teaching ministry.

That is not to say Tim's questions and conscious presence cannot also be forthright and pointed. Yet even as Tim speaks with unyielding honesty, the quality of his being conveys love simultaneous to any candid guidance he gives. Yet, beyond Tim or any particular personality in leadership, CCH is a living witness to what Divine love does to humankind when it comes close. It touches us and opens us, bringing healing and wholeness, deeper understanding and new ways of being. O how God loves us so.

∞

This introduction to Tim's sermons would be incomplete without mentioning Tim's wife Barbara, who graciously provided the foreword to this collection of sermons. As co-minister of CCH, Barbara's contribution to the depth of this spiritual community is visibly present as she leads the congregation in daily lectionary readings and Centering Prayer periods and retreats. Barbara's serenity, sincerity and love help anchor CCH retreats and worship, synthesizing scripture and practice in preparation for Tim's messages. Their ministerial marriage is evident each Sunday morning as Barbara and Tim sit beside each other in the front row, a visible testimony to the union of two bodies in service to Spirit. As you can imagine, over the years their ministry and marriage have unfolded in a very public dance, honestly including synchronicity, as well as the awkward moments stepping on each other's toes. An example of their love and partnership that illustrates this ever deepening union, is the oft repeated scene of Tim and Barbara walking arm in arm down the vestibule leading into the sanctuary before worship. Sometimes it seems as if they are harmoniously gliding into the church as one body, the golden fruit borne through many seasons soaking together in the light of Silence and Work.

I close this brief introduction with a prayer Tim often says at the beginning of the Wednesday evening worship service at CCH. It is a prayer that helps us move beyond the human resistance to love in our thinking. It aptly sums up the aim of this collection of sermons and prayers, and illustrates the indelible mark Tim's words have made on me, on you, and on all who will have ears to hear:

> "Most gracious and merciful, most wondrous God: We thank you for calling us and holding us together in your love while we grow. We thank you for the Life that we know is in your Word. Lord help us come open-minded, open-hearted and willing to be shown what it is we need to see to live the Life that you made us to live. We pray this in your Threefold Name: Father, Son, and Holy Spirit. Amen."

Part One:

The Contemplative Life

∞

One

Life and Suffering

∞

"There will be earthquakes in various places; there will be famines. This is but the beginning of the birth pangs." Mark 13.8

We are all going to die. So, in the end, it really becomes a matter of style: *how* am I going to die? Our church is about dying before we die. In Centering Prayer, we practice dying to the sense of a separate self. In the Work, we practice dying to the false personality, which is that ephemeral series of neural connections and habits of consciousness associated with small "l" life.

But the big "L" Life is deeper than that and it is here right now for us. Jesus referred to it as the "kingdom of heaven that is at hand" (Matthew 4.17). It is within us now. Through the spiritual practices that we do, through the participation in the silence and sacraments, through the community efforts and the support we get from one another, and through the daily study of scripture, Maurice Nicoll's *Psychological Commentaries* and our various community readings, we come more and more into expe-

riential awareness of the reality of *the* Life that is manifesting each of our particular lives.

In truth, each of us is a function of Christ within us – now
and always. Ever since the resurrection of Jesus, Christ
has been available to every human being right inside our
hearts. The challenge of the spiritual journey is how to get
our attention to go there even while we participate in the
world of affairs, do our shopping, pay our bills and have
our families. All of this "life" goes on as before, but the
feeling of "I," the feeling of my "I-am-ness" moves beyond
the surface-self and social masks that we wear, and into
the depths of being in the heart where God is "seated" on
the temple-throne that is each of our bodies.

So the spiritual journey is a journey not of distance, but a
journey of attention; a journey from the imprisoning head
into the heart. We are often caught in our thoughts. We
become identified with concepts gained from living in the
physical world, that is, until we come back to where we
started; back to the originating point of pure being in the
heart. Now not with the helplessness of an infant, or with
the childlike innocence that cannot do much in the
world, but now with the sophisticated capacities of a well-
trained adult who has regained the innocence and infinite
presence of the touch of God. So this is all we are about at
The Church of Conscious Harmony (CCH). We are about
returning ourselves to our Source and living the Life that
God has for us instead of the life that the world has been
teaching us.

I was trained in the Unity movement and was ordained as
a Unity minister, and these teachings of our deepest truth
are foundational to us. These are the teachings that

changed my life from a man controlled by external circumstances – always a victim – into an empowered person who learned to use the power of conscious thinking,
and conscious willing to serve aims that I had chosen instead of being driven by whims and urges, habits and situations. I learned to affirm the truth and to deny the er-
rors in my thinking. The fundamental truth of human life
is "thoughts held in mind, produce after their kind." The
thinking that we do becomes our circumstances. The
problem is that most of the thinking we do is unconscious. It is going on like a loaded gun that we are shooting without being aware that we are shooting. Clearly our
circumstances have something to do with our thinking.
When we learn to change our thinking and reprogram
ourselves we begin to have another kind of life entirely.

The problems we see in the world today are due to a lack
of balance and harmony. Human beings are out of sync
with their design specs. Human beings are running with
their sense of self "out there" in the world. Our wanting to
get things and wanting to change circumstances, in having grievances, all mean that our center of gravity has
been projected externally into areas that we have no influence over. This results in an internal vacuum into
which negativity can flow. We bail out of ourselves and
get lost in external conditions.

In the East it is called "names and forms" or the "Ten
Thousand Things." In life, there are endless things to get
identified with superficially and externally. If we do get
identified, there are perils and payments. There is always
a price for everything we do. When a human being lives
outside their design specs they will always experience
disharmony.

One caution in this kind of teaching is that as participants in a consumer culture, we are very susceptible to losing sight of God when we become empowered ourselves. We might say, "Look at me, I have got control. I am power-ful." We forget to glorify and praise the Source who not only lives us but makes liberating teachings available to us. If prayerful affirmations are done outside the context of the principle and command to "love the Lord your God with all your heart, and soul and mind and strength" (Luke 10.27) than you have wasted your time because you will still feel separate, even if you have a great deal of power or success. You have just become a self-improved or more healed separated person who is still living as if God is distant. So when miracles and moments of power happen, say, "O God, thank you for bringing me these teachings. Thank you for teaching me I do not need stress."

For example, I used to carry around a chronic feeling of worry about money. I got it from my parents. My dad survived a very difficult time during the Depression. His dad was so proud that he would not take welfare. So my dad went hungry sometimes. He had patches on his clothes. In fairness, he had experiential reasons to feel fear of lack of money and he communicated these fears to our family and to me. So, I dutifully carried on in my life as though there would not be enough money. Even when I had some I was always a little concerned about it. I had that feeling of angst, as if something was always about to go wrong. I always felt that way about money.

But, when I came to these empowering teachings, such as David Hawkings *Healing and Recovery,* I began to realize that I did not need that fear at all. God has been supplying me with everything I have ever needed. I do not need that feeling of anxiety. When I let go of the feeling, there was something in me that said, "If you put that down for a second, what if you cannot get it back?" The ludicrousness of these internal conversations struck me as being so bizarre that it is was an invitation to put that fear down. I have not had any concerns since. I tithe. God takes care of my money and God takes care of giving some to me. I praise God as my Source. I no longer need the fear of lack anymore. In a sense, I feel like I healed the family chain that went back to my dad and mom and my grandparents. I experienced in my own life the liberation that they could not have in theirs. I am standing on their shoulders. I am a flower on the stem of their hard efforts to get through life. Regarding prayer and suffering, we are in the realm of mystery. We are all engaged in this mystery. Prayer is not a simple cause and effect relationship. For example, there are also many times when people are not healed. There are many times when people bear things for years that seem to be afflictions that without fail turn into blessings. The difficulties we have to bear are ways in which Love inserts itself into our lives through challenges.

I have been healed of many things, including addiction to alcohol. I have also not been healed yet of the one thing that I would love to be healed of more than anything else. Yet, it has proven to be the greatest blessing of my life. So too was my cancer. My experience with cancer actually proved to be life giving. For my wife Barbara and me, it brought us together in a union of our spirits that we never could have had while I still thought I was brass plated and Teflon coated. I cannot explain why there is not a direct one-to-one cause and effect with our prayers and healing across the board. Affliction, if taken with God as a basis, always brings love. It makes for deeper love. Always.

The life that we experience appearing on the stage of history is not the whole of our lives. We are Life itself. We have always been alive and will never *not* be alive. The appearance and disappearance of our forms is almost irrelevant. What the Bible, mystics and sages of all ages have proclaimed to us is that you cannot die. You can cease to appear, but in clinging to the physicality and circumstances of our small "l" life we lose our big "L" life even while we are still wearing skin. To appear on the stage of history is not the fullness of our life. There is a depth and a presence in us that is eternal Life and you can have it now by doing practices that reduce the hold of the false self and the obscuring contents of the unconscious that mask and cover our big "L" Life. Christ within us is our hope of glory (Colossians 1.27). Not later, but now. Our true Life is "hidden with Christ in God" (Colossians 3.3).

Many people are eternally alive while still looking totally normal. They have the same Social Security number, same driver's license picture, but something is different in them. Their own life does not feel like their life anymore, it feels like God's Life now, and they live fearlessly. They live with delight and participate in the mystery of Life. They see the beauty in creation; they celebrate God instead of fearing all that consumes our cultural attention, stealing our true Life. At CCH, we teach a system of thinking and a system of experiencing our lives that we call the "Work" of Inner Christianity. This Work says, "Do not believe just because it is the custom to believe or because someone in authority says you should." The gospels are speaking not just of beliefs but of experiential realities. If we meet the gospels at the level of belief, we have sold ourselves short. Centering Prayer, the compendium of teaching that Thomas Keating has delivered, coupled with the Work of Inner Christianity, is a twofold path to the experience of Christ within.

Life as it is presented to us by the world is unsatisfactory to our hearts. We have to notice how we are asleep in false ideas; how we are incapable of intimacy in our friendships and relationships; how we have a chronic sense of anxiety deep in the pit of the belly; how the body is contracted and pulled in. What is going on here? When we begin to question our own lives then the Work of Inner Christianity can offer its transformative grace. These truths are not to be left in a book. They are things to be walked into life so that the Life God has made us for becomes the Life we are experiencing instead of the life that imitates the values of the world. Amen.[1]

∞

Two

Life and Oneness

∞

"You show me the path of life. In your presence there is fullness of joy; in your right hand are pleasures for evermore." Psalm 16.11

Sometimes it is said that God writes straight with crooked lines. Another way to say this is that we often do not see the coherence in our lives at the time difficult events are occurring, but later on we will. For example, in 1968 there was a young man who lived in Toronto who had discovered spirituality. He was getting every book he could on the subject. One day visiting a book shop that young man saw a book and was drawn to it. He picked it up, and then put it down. Picked it up, put it down and drove out of the bookstore driveway. The car stopped. He put the car into reverse, parked, went inside and bought the book. He drove to a park and all afternoon he read this book and a door opened in his heart; a change occurred in his being. The book was *Be Here Now* by Ram Das. This book was written at the Lama Foundation in San Cristobal, New Mexico in 1968.

I had no connection to the Lama Foundation then, but now, this year our young people will be going to the Lama

Foundation for their 9th annual pilgrimage. So it is amazing to see now how the hunger that was in a person's heart in 1968 went through a circuitous route; through all kinds of life changes to unfold into the gift of children from a church I would serve years later. At that time I did not even know I would be a minister!

Interestingly, the Lama Foundation was also the very first place Father Thomas Keating held his first Centering Prayer retreat. Countless other things have happened at the Lama Foundation that have changed the spiritual culture of at least the United States and, in my opinion, Western culture itself. It opened doors, not only to the spiritual relationship with God each individual person has, but it also began to break down some of the walls that separate various religions from one another.

My wife Barbara reminded me that in 1978 I did my first retreat at the Lama Foundation with Ram Das. I had no idea what I was getting into. I was a beginner, and like many beginners, I did not know what I did not know. There is much we do not know, but we never know how much we do not know or what specifically it is that we do not know, yet we find out what we do not know along the spiritual journey by what Father Keating calls a series of humiliations.

I had been reading spiritual books for ten years, and of course, I thought that made me "spiritual." I thought I knew everything, or at least I had a lot better vocabulary than what I had before, but I really did not know much at all. So I decided to go on retreat. I showed up at the Lama Foundation for a karma yoga retreat (at the time, I did not know what "karma yoga" meant). In the end, it turned out that it meant I was going to carry rocks for them, doing manual labor for the retreat center.

Now you will notice in my language that it was "them" and "us," "these guys" and "me." I thought to myself, "I paid my money damnit, so what am I carrying these rocks for?" I did not know what "internal considering" meant at that moment, but I now know it is the objections and rants that go on in the mind. I got to learn a great deal about what I thought was a loving mind in the silence as I carried rocks and had no distractions from my head. I got to see what an unloving guy I was at the time.

I was also in awe of Ram Das who wrote that amazing book, which, as I said, first opened the door to my heart. I will now share a story from that retreat, since it has such good, humiliating leverage on me, and it is always good to be re-humiliated.

On the last day of the retreat, Ram Das was walking up the hill as I was walking down. There was maybe 100 yards separating us. As we got closer and closer these thoughts were running through my head about what I would say. I did not know what to say but felt I needed to say something. So as we got nearer I said, "Hey old man that is some Kundalini you have got there." I did not even know what it meant, but I felt a blush go from toe to head and back down again. It was like the summary of all the humiliations of all the dumb things I had done in my life because it happened in silence, and there I was right in front of myself feeling stupid. Well, this type of thing has been repeated on countless occasions since then.

From the false self's point of view humiliation is awful. But from our being, this is how we get to the truth because the false self shows how bogus it is. It shows us it is just made of posturing and attempted impressions we are trying to deliver regarding what we want the world to think of us. Yet unless we are really having the experience we are trying to communicate, we are ripping ourselves off. These humiliations help us see what we are not, they help us let go and fall back into the truth that we are very dependent little creatures.

We are not at all the independent, self-actualizing beings we think ourselves to be. We are dependent on God for every heartbeat and every breath. We are dependent on God for the grace of friendship and for leading us every moment of every day. It is God who satisfies the hungers of our heart, and who, situation after situation, teaches us the truth that ultimately makes us free. I am so grateful God wrote straight with these crooked lines of my life. I am so grateful that the hunger I had has ultimated in the gift of this community.

There is another loving story that happened while I was at Lama. In the ceramics shop we made chalices for ourselves and fired them in the kiln. On the last day of the retreat we gathered under the full moon and had communion using the cups we made. The entire group of 80 people stood in a circle in the moonlight singing spiritual songs and praying together. I had feelings that I had never experienced before; feelings that I liked and had always wanted to feel. I felt whole and enriched by the good company of fellow spiritual pilgrims. Because I was a loner at the time, I was scared of people and very shy. Yet suddenly and unexpectedly I experienced the gift of community.

After the circle broke up, I stayed out under the moon-light praying. I said, "God I want community. I want this. I want to be part of such a thing." The hunger of that heart has ultimated in our being here today at The Church of Conscious Harmony (CCH). The great mystery of God's oneness revealed through that very strange look-ing book that I was attracted to in 1968 in a book shop in Toronto has resulted in more depth with the Lama Foun-dation than I could have ever imagined.

The Lama Foundation was one of the first intentional communities in the country and it has survived all the tugs and pulls customary to such community life. It is difficult building community because there are disparate ways of seeing and being. How do you make room for everybody to be fully human, to bear their ordinary hu-manity and yet still have rules that guide the community with intention and focus? That of course is a delicate art.

For us, the Christian way has given us the great gift of being in the body of Christ. As members of the body of Christ, we feel Christ holding our individualities while we bear our separate selves – our false selves – and we bear each other's personalities. The Work tells us that we are to bear both our pleasant and unpleasant manifestations.

Over the 22 years our CCH community has grown deeper and deeper because God has held us in place while we grow. God has held us in relationship. God lets us build community, and all the time the whole group has been surrendered to God. God has been the principal focus of our lives, and what a gift we have been given.

Recently, Bernadette Roberts was with us for three days. Bernadette was our very first retreat master 22 years ago. I had been following her around just picking up the bread crumbs for several years. She was the one who said, "You need to go back to Austin. Your friends are there and you need to start a work down there."

When that work got off the ground, we invited her to be our first retreat master. I was so eager for our friends to get what she was offering. But nobody got it! In fact, they were actively angry at her. To be fair, she is a very challenging teacher, and of course challenging is not what we want. We like our comfort. We do not want to have to do away with our solid, firm categories. Anything that causes us to challenge our own thinking or that causes us to examine ourselves deeply and find out that there is only mystery here and that we are really not explicable can be wildly unpopular.

Last week we had 70 people that stayed with Bernadette the entire three days and it was evident that many of those people understood what she was offering. What she is offering is so simple, yet so universal and so radical that it is almost unbelievable. In fact, Thomas Keating says, "the truth is literally unbelievable." You cannot believe it. You can experience it, but it is not believable, because belief is an intellectual ascent to something.

The truth of what Bernadette is teaching is the truth of "no self," a concept that has been around in Buddhism for years. Christianity, in its earliest development, was clearly coming from that same place. But having inherited Greek thought forms, Christianity submitted to Greek rationalistic categories. The Greeks tended to be dualistic in their thinking and as a result Christianity took a decisively dualistic turn in its development. The problem with this was that Western dualistic rationalism was never the intended basis of Christianity. Its basis and being was faith.

Most of us have inherited some form of dualistic Christianity. Whether we know it intellectually or not, it is just how it feels: like God is somewhere else, God is over there somewhere. We often think that Jesus has gone away somewhere else, but we are still here. Rabbi Avi says, "Form is empty and emptiness is form." This is exactly what the ancient fundamental Christian teaching is as it is expressed in the gospel according to John, "In the beginning was the Word, and the Word was with God and the Word was God, and from Him all things came to be and not one thing that was came to being outside of Him" (John 1.1-2). This is not dualistic. It is wholeness.

The Word is emptiness; it is not a thing. It is the Source of things, as the ocean is the source of all waves. The waves are one with the ocean, but they do not own the whole ocean. You and I are particular expressions of the divine Infinity. We are waves on an ocean of existence. Can you feel the ocean of existence? The all-ness that contains the galaxies? The sun, the moon, everything on Earth? Absolutely everything is in that all-ness, the ocean of existence. Here little human waves rise up; they come for their three score and ten. They persist for a while and then they fall back. They appear, persist and then disappear.

A materialist would say that when something is not here, it is gone. That if it appears for a while and then disappears, we have lost it. In fact in medical language we will hear people say, "We lost him." Gone? Is he gone? The Paramitra Sutra says, "Gone where?" Gone beyond, that is where. Gone beyond the world of things and facts. But did the ocean disappear? Of course not.

Recently we began to read from Rami Shapiro's book called *Open Secrets*. This book is a series of letters that Rami's grandfather wrote from European Russia to his teacher asking spiritual questions. When I came across this book I was dumbfounded because I had never seen Jewish writing like this. In our early years together, Barbara and I studied with a Rabbi for a couple of years. We were studying the Kabbalah. So, when we read *Open Secrets*, we sent it to our former Rabbi. He wrote back saying, "No Jew in 18th century Russia ever thought like that." But, obviously there was and we were reading his profound teaching in Rami's book.

As it turns out Rami Shapiro, the author of *Open Secrets* is a friend of Thomas Keating. Rami is to the Jewish world what Thomas is in the Christian world, open and receptive to all the traditions and yet firmly grounded in his own. Thomas is all Christian but he embraces the religions of the world. Rami is all Jewish and yet he embraces all the religions of the world. Our church was founded on the principle that while we are firmly planted on our Christian roots, we seek and accept illumination and insight from the great religions and traditions of the world always with a view to enliven our own practice to our Christian faith.

You might see the great religions as languages by which the particulars (i.e. people) try to get in touch with the Infinite One. How do we speak to the Infinite Presence and how do we relate to it so that it is a two-way exchange? How do we avoid feeling alienated, separated and cut-off from the whole thing? The great religions have developed in response to that need. Our tradition is a revelation that comes from God's side to ours, in which the one God has revealed Godself to Abraham, Isaac, Jacob, Moses, Joseph, David, Solomon, John the Baptist, Jesus and right on up to this day. It is the same Reality that is expressing itself in Judaism, in Buddhism, in all the great religions of the world. The One Reality never changes just because someone else speaks a different language.

Certain languages allow certain expressions to be made more easily. French, I am told, has a lot of subtlety to it that we do not have in English. Our English language is cruder. When we can begin to understand the universal thread that runs through all of these religions, we begin to understand our own even better.

Here are a few more examples of this unspeakable mystery: Thirty spokes make up a wheel, but it is the emptiness in the center that makes it functional. We also have talked about a bowl. A bowl has a form but it is the emptiness in it that lets it be of any use at all. Likewise a house is a solid, but it is the empty windows and doors that give it functional utility. So we say a human being is a play of emptiness and form: the form of our being and the emptiness of our spirits. I can see your shape and you can see mine, but I cannot see your spirit. Only you have access to your deep interior realms. We are invisible to each other. And though we comment on each other's shape and form, and though that is the usual extent of our awareness of other people, what we see with our senses is not who or what we are.

We feel ourselves spiritually. We feel ourselves in the invisible realms. So a human being is an interplay between emptiness and form; between fact and universality; between spirit and matter; between time and eternity. The Hebrew words were *Yesh*, meaning being or facticity, and *Ayin*, or emptiness. Visible and invisible. Matter and energy. Form and formless. Time and eternity. These are all aspects of the intersection of that which moves and that which is moved, of that which appears and that which does not appear. It is the invisible that manifests and moves the visible. It is the ocean that manifests and moves each wave. There is no wave without the ocean, and no ocean without the waves. But the ocean comes first. It is almost like Jesus saying, 'The Father and I are one" (John 10.30).

Although the wave and the ocean are one, remember that Jesus said, "the Father is greater than I" (John 14.28). It is like a wave saying, "The ocean and I are one but the ocean is greater than I." In each of us, behind our thoughts, deeper than our feelings and sensations is pure Life. That Life we have come to understand is the risen Christ as personal Presence within us with infinite capacity to bless and manifest wonders; to change things; to heal, to bring joy in the midst of what seems like sorrow and to bring peace in a chaotic world. What keeps us from feeling that joy and living from it? We do. We keep looking at the waves and comparing them to other waves. We are criticizing and judging waves, having forgotten that the ocean is the absolute necessity for any of the waves to be here at all!

For those of us who would just as soon forget the waves and notice only the ocean, we have to understand that it does not work that way. We are here to participate in the blessed dance between the co-created parts of the whole. When Christ tells us to "love one another as I have loved you" (John 13.34-35), we are being informed that the ocean loves all the waves, and each wave should love both the ocean and all the other waves too in order to be real.

If we want to be real, we have to notice that we are not in this by ourselves, nor are we making ourselves happen. Keep in mind that scientists have divided the second into 1 billion parts called "nanoseconds." Yet, long before scientists accomplished this, Buddhist mediators were able to see 69 parts in a second. Thus, scientific observation confirms our human multiplicity of experience. In light of this, remember *Yesh* and *Ayin*, the wave and the ocean, the visible and invisible.

Paralleling this is another analogy. In quantum physics, we might call the "ocean" the field. It is the great field of all being in which things come and go, appear and disappear. That is the ocean and we are a part of that field, which can also be called the body of Christ. When we are aware of ourselves as facts we forget the ocean. When we see ourselves as manifestations we forget the field. There really is not a specific, definite, cut-out object called "you." You are really blinking on and off 1 billion times a second.

Physicists have also shown us that even this very dense stone on this table is vibrating very rapidly at the atomic level. The wood in these beams is vibrating. Everything is vibrating. We are at an intersection with reality that makes it look solid because our senses are vibrating at the same rate as the materiality around us. We know there are many layers of vibrations that are extra sensory and sub-sensory. There is a whole spectrum of wavelengths of which human experience intersects just a small section.

If our attention gets locked into a particular perception, we forget the greater whole we are living in. We might call such forgetting the life of sin. It does not mean we are bad people doing something wrong. Rather, we are living in error, we are living as if God is not real. We are living as if God is not here. God is here. God is always here. We would not be here if God were not here. Instead of seeing ourselves as things that appeared decades ago that will disappear in a while, let us experience ourselves as continuing manifestations of the energetic spectrum continuously appearing as waves on the ocean, but always coexisting with the ocean. There is no me without God; no God without me.

When the wave gets embarrassed of its waveness, it may for a second discover its oceanness. When we see ourselves in the light of truth as inexplicable, we cannot explain ourselves. We cannot figure out how we got here or how we persist or how breathing or metabolism happens. It is all a big mystery. So we may, in that moment, intuit and let go into the presence of God.

Bernadette Roberts says that humankind, as we were originally created, has his/her center in God. It is part and parcel of our being, without which we could not exist. But we displace this center by putting our self at the center. When by grace the self is displaced (as happens in the dark night), we once more recognize God as our true center, a recognition that is not just conceptual or a mere matter of belief, but one that comes through experiential contact.

Grace is the means by which we return to our original, unitive center. We can think of this union as supernatural, but in truth the means is not the end. Our end is the same as our beginning: union with God. We were babies imbedded in God and then we forgot. We were wavelets, still one with the ocean, and then we got concerned with our waviness. Our original union with God is the end, like the beginning, which is in turn the very same union realized by a contemplative in the unitive state who has become aware of herself or himself as both wave and ocean at the same time.

The separate self-sense is what the common culture says is true of us. We are consumers. We are statistics, economic indicators. We are facts and little particulars. The mystics and contemplatives, sages and saints, and especially Jesus revealed that there is only One here and that it is all One Christ. There is no separate self. There never has been a separate self: it is an appearance, a deceptive appearance at that, because when we attend only to that separate self sense, only to our waveness, we completely forget about the ocean.

We then feel bereft and long for meaning and feel loss of peace. We do not have joy. Where will our joy come from in our union with God? From the joy of being a wave on the ocean of life and letting the great ocean manifest us. We will feel joy from the privilege of dancing with the other waves and for participating consciously in the great mystery of existence. We can feel the play between invisibility and visibility, between time and eternity, between facts and the universe of Being. There is only one here – one life and one humanity. No individual persists. Just as we blink on and off a billion times a second, so does everybody else. We are really dotted lines more than we are hard outlines. There is no separate self (c.f., James 4.14).

I remember some 20 years ago being on retreat with Bernadette and listening as hard as I could. My brain was burning trying to understand her. Finally I said, "Are you saying that there is no individual?" And she said, "There is no individual. There is Christ." Listen, Jesus says things like: "What you do to the least of these my brethren, you do to me. What you do not do for these, you do not do for me (Matthew 25.31ff). I am in you and you are in me, and we are in the Father" (John 14.2). There is no separate self; there is Christ. We can know it now, or we can know it at the end of our days.

The joy of knowing it *now* is that we get to dance with our creator for the rest of our days, fearlessly filled with love in our hearts, undefended and active in the mystery, trusting in God always to lead and guide us from good to greater good. Just as a young man was guided in 1968 to pick up a book that led him to something else, that led him to this church, each of us can trust our lives to the great ocean of existence and let the invisible part of us be the truth that keeps us free even while the facts of our lives go on happening.

The joy of knowing God, the joy of letting God have us back is the most amazing gift we could ever have. It is counter-cultural. We will not get complimented for it. We probably will never be recognized for it. We will not care because we will be too busy enjoying the ocean's manifestations and trusting it to do what is right with all its waves. Amen.[2]

∞

Three

Life in the World

∞

"Make a joyful noise to the LORD, all the earth; break forth into joyous song and sing praises." Psalm 98.4

When we are confronted by apocalyptic texts like these that seem to predict things that are going to happen in the future, or that speak of God's wrath and fury, it is wise to take a pause and put the texts aside. We can then mull over their mysterious presentation of rich symbology, moving the text into relationship with something we can know about directly. When we take such texts literally we often end up with more confusion than what we first started out with.

Thus, to help us in reducing our confusion, we will begin with the law of analogy. One of the greatest pieces of ancient wisdom is the law of analogy, such as, "That which is above is as that which is below." What this maxim is teaching us is that if you can see in microcosm how things work you can intuit how the macrocosm, or the greater whole works. We will use this principle to look into these mysterious texts.

Here is an example. We know that human beings are microcosms created in the image and likeness of the Creator. If we want to know something about the Creator we can look at our own structures and begin with simple observations to move into a deeper understanding of things that are presented to us in symbolic language. For example, take the structure of our human body. We have skin which is present in three layers. There is the epidermis, which is in contact with the outer world and there is the mesoderm, which is between the epidermis and the inner layer called the endodermis. So the epidermis is in touch with the outside. The endodermis is in touch with the inside, and the mesoderm is in between. Here we see, in part, a structural trinity: three unique parts making up one skin, but its oneness is comprised of threeness.

Now let us look at human development. When a baby is born and we look into the baby's eyes we see clearly that there is a unique human being there. I remember looking into my granddaughter's newborn eyes. It was astonishing. I saw a person looking back at me. There was no content, or even the slightest bit of experience of this world in her perception, and yet there was a full human being confronting me.

There I was with all my definitions, all my knowledge, all my experience weaved together into a story called "my life," and yet what I saw before me was Life itself. It did not have a "my" part yet. It did not have a possessive ownership, but it was Life! You could say that my infant granddaughter, at that moment, was all interiority. There was no exteriorization of her attention or feeling of self at all.

So, when we are looking at the baby we are looking back at the Infinite. As that Life looks out and sees the world it has come into, it has no capacity to interact with it – yet. No capacity to exchange – yet. In human development, as the soul is formed by its experiences in life, something develops that begins to have its own life. That soul then begins to interact with the world and forgets about the deep interior whence it came. It forgets about that indescribable Source that seems so mysterious even little kids are astounded by it.

From such original innocence, we are thrust out into the world. We reach outside ourselves and get caught in what the book of Revelation refers to as "the beast." The beast is that vast, circulation of recurring human experience that goes on and on, generation after generation: of war, greed, violence, oppression and persecution. The beast is what is called the fallen world. The beast is the one that exists all by itself, like a current of energy, sweeping human beings out of their interiority and into identification with the circumstances outside of them.

In order to become God's people, in order to live in harmony with Truth and Life, there has to be a return journey. The identity has to extract itself from the physicality of war, pestilence, persecution, difficulties of every sort, and find itself again in that place of innocence and perfection that we were born with. Jesus said, "You will not enter the kingdom of heaven unless you enter it as a child" (Matthew 18.3), or with the mind of a child. Where did Jesus tell us the kingdom of heaven was? Within. It is at hand. It is within you right now (Luke 17.21). The great difficulty with scripture is that it tends to make us look somewhere else, but the reason it is scripture is that it is speaking to all people, in all circumstances at all times, in their *nowness*. Inevitably layers of varnish have been put on since the scriptures were first expressed that make it very difficult to get at the core of its interior meaning except by using things such as the law of analogy.

Similarly, just like skin, human beings have a deep interiority that can be thought of as our endodermis. The deep interiority is the mystery as far back as your attention can go inward. You will go deeper and deeper into the mystery, into the light that appears to us as darkness because it is so bright it makes us blind. This is the pure light of God – undiminished by the screens of thought, the screens of logic, screens of expectation and resistance. This is the light, the pure, uncreated light of God.

Thus we have an interior section that is "my life" or "my interior thoughts." We also have the exterior world that we are attached to and identified with in various ways. If we are to become God's people, we have to learn to let go of that. We need to let go of our addictions, our attachments and our condemnations. Remember, Jesus said, "Judge not lest ye be judged" (Matthew 7.1ff) and "Forgive if you want to be forgiven" (Luke 6.37).

The whole of the fifth and sixth chapter of Matthew is about letting go of the world and the way the world is commonly experienced. For example, "Love your enemies." "Pray for those that curse you." "Love those that spitefully use you." "Go the extra mile." "Turn the other cheek." "Give them your coat too." In light of our reading from Revelation, God's fury is the energy that we have inherited from all the undigested karmic nonsense of previous lifetimes. If people get caught in it, it is a horrible energy. It swallows people up. To get out of it and to come back into the depths of being whence we came, we have to begin to let go. This letting go, for those of us who have experienced unloading in the spiritual journey, is not just, "Well I am going to let go now." It is difficult.

Thomas Keating reminds us that "the false self does not just fall over and play dead just because we are ready to go back to God." It sets up an awful struggle. The struggle is not one with a living creature, but rather one with the tendency of mechanical habits, both psychologically and spiritually. We are habituated to our familiar and comfortable ways of doing, knowing, judging, fearing, clinging, attaching and dividing. These familiar habits are neurologically ingrained into our neural nets. To get the energy to go out of them requires us to do something that is more powerful than those habits.

There is help for our situation in the sacrament of the Eucharist. The Lord's Supper trumps everything. Also, in the Word we have something that overcomes all our struggles. Yet the false self has to be trumped not only just once and for all, but over and over and over, day after day, situation after situation, as we choose to know that our true Life is not out there. Our Life is not in our thoughts and feelings, but in the deepest interiority where God speaks us into existence from the unutterable silence, from infinite love, and utter, undoubtable Presence. Our true Life is "hidden with Christ in God" (Colossians 3.3).

This return journey is fraught with struggles. These struggles are enumerated in the gospel according to Luke. Listen to this as if it were all occurring within one individual.

A microcosmic look of what the macrocosm is like. This is what the false self is actually doing to an individual: "They will seize you and persecute you and hand you over to the synagogues and prisons. They will lead you before kings and governors because of my name" (Luke 12.10-12).

The minute we start to get ahold of that name, and let it get ahold of us, the minute we start to give our allegiance to that interior consciousness, every one of our old habits jumps up and starts to make claims on us. They testify against us saying, '"You are stupid to believe in God. You are stupid for letting go of your resistance to evil. You are stupid for turning the other cheek. You are just a patsy."

Inner voices start to tell us that we are stupid and foolish. They lead us before interior authorities. They will even use such things as the Bible to quote scripture to us in a twisted fashion to make us think that what we are doing is really justified. We might hear something like: "I am going to fix it." Yet Jesus says: Remember, you are not to prepare your defense beforehand for I myself will give you wisdom in speaking that all your adversaries will be powerless to resist or refute.

Where are our adversaries? They are interior. Read John's gospel. What does he call the liar and the father of lies? The adversary – that which is against me is the accuser. If there is some accusing going on in the inner courts of our heart and mind, if there is adversarialness going on inside, you can be sure that is the accuser. That is what is called "the devil." It has the accuser's fingerprints all over it. It will try to convince you that letting go of your hold on the world – either a resisting one or a grabbing one – is the worst thing you could possibly do. The beast wants you to stay attached. The circulating energy wants to eat people. The more people give it their attention, the more power the beast has.

Another example of the microcosmic view of this dynamic is the example of football. It has a tremendous energetic field around it. The more fans it has who give attention to it, the more that energy exists and grows. For example, all the people who are UT fans corporately and collectively create the energy field around UT. If it only had two fans, it would not be that way. It is similar for the beast, as it is spoken of in reading from Revelation. The circulating, recurring energy field that sucks people in wants every single one of us to stay attached because it feeds on our energy. It is very much like the movie *The Matrix* where the system lives on people. When people start to let go, their own conditioning tries to keep them attached to it. It hypnotizes us into thinking our lives are "out there" instead of in here.

So Jesus says, "You will even be handed over by parents, brothers, relatives and friends." I cannot tell you how many people I have counseled who go on the spiritual journey and whose family members do not think contemplation is a good idea. I knew a monk who got letters from his brother saying, "This is a waste of your life. Here you are an educated man who could do some good for the world and you have taken yourself out of the mainstream to do what? Sit in silence and work on a farm?" Such are the kinds of tugs and pulls our own family conditioning often pressures us with.

But here is the promise, "You will be hated by all." This is not talking about our biological brother or parent. It is the image of the brother or parent within us that we carry inside. It is the expectation of a combat that holds us locked in, "You will be hated by all of your conditionings because of my name," because of Christ's name in your heart. Nothing in us wants to let go of that personal and cultural identity we have gained in the time since we were born. Nothing in us wants to let go of chasing after the carrot and the stick. Every bit of our conditioning will struggle against Christ within, yet when we do, we re-claim our lives and in fact it is revealed that our life has never been our own – it is Christ's.

I am the way, he said. I am Truth. I am Life (John 14.6). If we find the Life in us, we have found Christ. If we have found the Life in us we have found Truth, and it is itself the way. When we call ourselves into that way more and more deeply, there is a struggle for every bit of it. But Jesus says, "Do not worry about a thing. Not a hair on your head will be destroyed, because by your perseverance you will secure your lives." Another translation says, "You will save your souls."

Our dilemma is that the soul (i.e., the *psyche*) can get attached and become identified with the outer world. Yet its true home is within. To return to our initial skin anal-ogy, Christ is the middle term between the outside world and the Spirit within. If we stay attached to Christ our mediator, and move within with our attention, there will be struggles of course, but the new man and the new woman is ready to be born (2 Corinthians 5.17-21). The mind of Christ wants to take its place instead of our minds. We will arrive at the place where we can join with Paul saying, "Now not I live, but Christ in me" (Galatians 2.19-20). This is the promise to each of us who is willing to go on the journey back to the Source. Do you hunger for meaning and the peace that passes understanding? Do you hunger for being joyful? Remember what Christ said: "I came that you might have joy. That my joy might be in you and your joy complete" (John 15.11).

Are the captains of industry really having a good time with all their power? Do those who make profits off munitions and arms sales really sleep that well at night? Yet regardless of their lack of conscience, that is not who they really are in essence. They are asleep, lost in what Revelation calls the swirling mirage of the beast. It circles generation after generation, sweeping them up into its vortex, telling them that their identity is somehow in things, in concepts or accomplishments. In contrast, our identity is in our hearts, in Christ who is always here, always calling to us, "Follow me. Pick up your cross and follow me in the regeneration of the human species. Follow me to the new life that you are hungry for." Paul says that all of creation is groaning with inexpressible longings, waiting for the daughters and the sons of God to be born. Why is it groaning? We are groaning because it is aching with the pain of being separated from the truth.

We all ache when our identity is turned outward instead of inward. But the journey home is a safe journey. We have been guaranteed safe passage by our perseverance. What does that look like? It looks like sitting in the morning and evening in Centering Prayer, where we are opened by the Spirit to listen for God's first word in the silence, participating in the sacraments, studying the scriptures, letting *Lectio Divina* teach us the words and phrases that give us insights we did not have before. God is a perfectly reliable shepherd and the world is a perfectly unreliable resource. It is a question of who do you choose to follow today. It is not an all-or-nothing game. Our aimlessness is perfectly taken into account. We are not expected to become saints overnight. But if our intention and attention are not directed interiorly, we are making an error of navigation. The truth is within us, and the truth will be met one day or another. We are going to put these bodies down some day and graduate from this realm of experience. What the contemplative learns to do is to die before she dies. Dying, like that grain of wheat Jesus speaks of so that each of us might be born as Christ's own person. This is the destiny of each of us if we choose to accept it. Know that there are angels and guardians helping all along the way.

Struggles? Of course there are struggles in the inner forums of consciousness. Of course there are bargains to broker with the ideals of how life ought to be, but Christ within is our hope of glory, infallibly the truth, the way, our very own Life. We can trust Christ a lot more than we can trust the unreliable beast. The world itself is not a bad place, but rather, it is what people do in it. In the 17th chapter of John's gospel Jesus is praying, saying, "Lord, I ask, not that you take them out of the world, but that you keep them safe from the evil one while they are in it" (John 17.15). So, we are not going to withdraw from culture. We are not going to stop being humans in society. What we are going to take back is our identity. Our identity belongs to God and it is right within us – within our heart.

Our field of soul-growth is in learning to practice love even while we remain in the world. We grow as we live out the values of the Beatitudes and the values of the

Sermon on the Mount, even while we are appearing in human form amongst peoples who have no idea that we are doing this and could not care less. This is our great destiny: to practice this while we are still alive. It is not that the world is bad and that we are going to hurl a curse on it. We just have to know that it is pretty sticky here. Remember, every time you stick your hand into the hive to grab honey it comes out with bee stings, right through all three layers of your Trinitarian skin. Hmmm. Amen.[3]

∞

Four

Life in Christ

∞

"All the paths of the LORD are steadfast love and faithfulness, for those who keep his covenant and his decrees."
Psalm 25.10

I grew up in the Midwest and one of my favorite times I had as a kid was when snowstorms would cripple the city and neighbors would help each other out. I especially remember how people helped push stuck cars out of snow banks. In those situations, I noticed a feeling of community that otherwise never seemed to happen. This phenomena is also seen played out on a bigger scale when there is an earthquake or natural tragedy where people are in trouble and others immediately show up to help. In moments of great crisis, we know ourselves as a body of humankind in a way that transcends our separate individuality. We seem to be able to easily help each other out in extreme situations. I have also noticed that it is in the ordinary moments that we have difficulty relating to each other as a community and as a living body.

I have never seen this more dramatically demonstrated than in coal mine disasters. In coal mine disasters, media from all over the world arrives so to provide updates on how the rescue is going. The entire world gets mobilized around some miners trapped underground. One such rescue happened in Pennsylvania a few years ago. The rescuers bored a whole into the earth for several days in order to reach the trapped men, all the while hoping that the trapped miners had enough air to stay alive.

When the hole the engineers bored proved to be worthy they enlarged it. Finally, after nearly a week, the hole was ready and they dropped in a rescue cage on the end of a cable into which each individual miner could step and be lifted back up to the surface. The media intensity and the general feeling of being part of a globalized rescue event kept our attention aware of the situation. People would talk about the miners in stores and there seemed to be a general awareness of this disaster and of the intention to rescue those lost.

So by analogy, here is the human race caught in a mine disaster. The human condition has collapsed in upon itself and we have lost touch with the air and surface above – the breath of Spirit. Amazingly, humankind seems relatively unconcerned about our predicament. We do not realize what Mr. Gurdjieff called "the terror of the situation." The good news is that God knows this and helps us.

The human condition is one in which we are caught in a terrible play of separation in which I feel separate from you and you feel separate from me, and we feel separate from our good – from that which our souls are hungry for. So we go on about our business of setting up societies

that attempt to alleviate that cramp and sense that something is not right, that something is wrong. To alleviate
the discomfort, we invent remedies and appeasements to
ourselves and God in an attempt to do something about
our sense of alienation – sexual, philosophical, psychological and scientific. Chances are we have tried all of these
ways to address this feeling of alienation, but God in love
has sent in a means of rescue. God sent in a means of our
escape. Just like the cage that the engineers sent down to
the trapped miners so that they could get into it and be
lifted up to the surface, so too there is a vehicle for us.
There are multiple versions of that vehicle, yet all of them
are God reaching into our world, our cut-off separative
feeling, offering us a way to come into Life.

The Eucharist is one way God is offering us help. God
feeds us with God and in so doing God is really taking us
into divine Life. We are also fed with God's Word and are
invited to get into the Word so to be lifted out of our circumstances. But that is the difficult part for us. The miners had no difficulty realizing when the rescue cage came
down that they wanted to be in it and be lifted up to the
surface. They were not at all confused about the desper-
ateness of their situation and so they did not need to be
coached or coaxed. Nothing needed to be done except for
them to stand in the cage and be lifted up from above.

Yet how different it is for us! O what effort it takes for us
to get into the Word. We do not really have a sense of our
mortality or of our desperate need for rescue. We can ra-
tionalize and put it off. We can accommodate ourselves
to the stale air and dark conditions of culture. We accept
breathing the spirit of society, even though it makes us
nauseated. We are able to go on because the crowd does,

but all along there is a different, higher Life available to us. Receiving this Life takes an act of will on our part. We must choose to step into the escape strategy that God offers us, which is Christ. God invites us to step into understanding that there is a savior who came to save the world from itself; who came to save us from this awful dream that we are separate from God, from our good and each other.

To get into this salvation mechanism with Christ reveals us to be dissatisfied with the stale air of life. We are dissatisfied with the darkness. We are dissatisfied with the feelings of alienation from our Source who is goodness itself. If we are dissatisfied with those things, please know that the savior is speaking to us so we can say and know that the Messiah has come. Christ is the Way back to where the air is good; to the Life that was ours before we fell asleep under the powerful spell of separation.

Notice that when the Sadducees approach Jesus in the text from Mark's gospel asking about small points of the law, that they are not – to continue the analogy – the slightest bit interested in climbing into the rescue basket. They are interested in being powerful and feeling in control. They want to get the religious formula just right so that they can do for themselves what needs to be done. They want to be the guys in charge of their lives. But to get into this basket Jesus offers, you have got to give up being in charge of your life. You have to give up being in control or of knowing what and who is "right." You simply come to God in need. There is no heroic overcoming of one's own limitations. It is all grace. Yet to receive this grace we have to surrender all our self-bound efforts to raise ourselves from the level of the human condition and let God raise each one of us.

The Jewish tradition that informs the Christian concept of the messiah is a tradition that was evolving toward the messiah from the very beginning. It was a tradition in which God is interactively related to the human race, offering revelations of divine presence to humankind. God offers us a means by which we might respond. Thus, God offers the Law, and Israel is given the opportunity to relate to God through the Law helping people aim toward the truest and deepest good. God gave the prophets who offered a way to truth and justice. And God inspired profound prayers. For example, the Psalms are a most wondrous example of one of the gifts God has given us. Prayerful ways for us to get into the cage of deliverance that lifts us up out of our self and into the connected Life of God: "The Lord is my refuge, my shield and the strength of my salvation" (Psalm 18.2).

Today we have been given quantum mechanics that explains a lot of the same stuff we are addressing in the Bible. Quantum mechanics tells us that the thought forms and intentions that human beings have, can and do shape the quantum field – the interior of me has something to do with the exterior of me. The kind of attention I give to certain things becomes manifest. You might say that this human creative mechanism is loaded, and God through the Psalms is teaching us how to use it.

The Psalms help us shape our own expectations of God through our thoughts and intentions. We are shaping our own understanding of God with our own intentions. Our expectations of God become effectively God for us. If we think we need to manipulate, fear or appease God, that expectation is itself creating a certain kind of relationship with the All and Everything. But God has sent some words uttered through the Psalmist David, and these words are really offered to us as an invitation, saying, "You can approach me this way too." Let us look at one Psalm in particular: "In you I trust, let not me be put to shame. Let not my enemies exalt over me" (Psalm 25.2).

Right away we see that these words are beginning to condition the cosmic field. It is in "you" I trust. The Psalmist is not trusting in himself. It is in God that I trust. "Let not my enemies exalt over me." What then are the enemies? They are our thoughts and emotions, negative things that keep assailing us with messages that say God is not here. After I have conditioned the field by saying who I trust in, now I can say what I want: I do not want my enemies to prevail over me. The universe operates in response to request. God is teaching us how to request in a way that will bring a perfect response to us.

The Psalm continues: "No one who waits for you will be put to shame. Those will be put to shame who heedlessly break faith." The Psalmist is telling himself that I am not going to break faith with God and I will not be put to shame because I am waiting for God. The Psalmist continues: "Your ways O Lord, make known to me. Teach me your paths. Guide me in your truth and teach me, for you are God my savior." We announce the fact that God is our savior. This obliges God to do the saving and it gets the person doing the praying out of the position of having to do something for ourselves that ultimately cannot be done and that we have to trust God for.

Again: "Remember that your compassion and your kindness are from old." It has always been this way. "In your kindness, not in your vengeance, not in your wrath, not in your judgment, but in your kindness Lord, remember me because of your goodness." Reminding ourselves that the Lord is goodness and kindness helps us to begin to expect from God, not the culturally defined pattern which often brings conflict, separation, alienation, pain and death, but goodness. Again: "Good and upright is the Lord, thus he shows sinners the way." Do you know any sinners? There is nothing bad about being a sinner. Everybody is a sinner who thinks and lives as though they are separate from God. You show sinners the way. I can trust that you are going to show me the way, Lord.

Furthermore: "He guides the humble to justice and teaches the humble his way." What is humility? It is knowing your place. Where is my place? It is total dependence on God. Trusting God. Giving myself to God as often as I forget and go my own way. Humility is the willingness to come back, because when I am gone from God I am missing out on true Life, taking sleep for being awake – this is exactly where God comes to rescue me from my sleep and spiritual death.When filled with thoughts about myself, including criticisms, I am dead. I am nothing but emotional reactivity and intellectual reflections about various possibilities. In such a state, I am a walking imagination machine. The minute I realize my dependence on God and physical mortality, I will become aware of God as answering my prayers. In that moment, I am alive because God comes to save me right then and there. God is not the God of the dead but of the living. And I am a creation of the living. When God is real, I am real. When God is not real, I am not real. Thus, sin is the unreality of God and this is exactly why Jesus came to save us from sin. How simple. So simple that Jesus said it would take a child's mind to get it. The Sadducees with all their reasoning and materially based sense consciousness were intent on staying that way. Those who come to Life must know they are not alive and those who would be saved must know they need saving because then they can ask the Savior, and Christ will save them not just later, but right here and now. This is the miracle of divine rescue.

How many times do we fall back down into the mine? We probably fall countless times a day. How many times does God come down to rescue us? Every time we are willing to step into the rescue vehicle which is for us the Word, the Eucharist, Centering Prayer, and our application of the Work ideas. All of these graces have been given to us in order to release us from the bondage of the human condition. It is easy to be convinced that the Life Christ is offering to us is a good deal with all that is going on in the world and in our bodies that does not feel right. That feeling is from "bad air." That is to say, from living in the darkness.

Thus Jesus says to the Sadducees, "How greatly do you err. You do not know the scriptures." If we are telling stories to ourselves with the scriptures or carrying them around and knowing them, but never let them change or rescue us, how greatly do we miss the mark. The scriptures are the doorway to eternal Life and this Life is here right now and forever. Amen.[4]

∞

Five

Life in Evolution

∞

"I still have many things to say to you, but you cannot bear them now." John 16.12

We often take our dogs for a walk at Common's Ford Ranch. As we are walking the trails, we find fossils, and in particular a fossil called *protocardia*. It is a fossil of one of the first kind of heart shaped clams. It was natures' first shot at making a heart shape form – *proto*, meaning first and *cardia*, meaning heart. Long before there was any thought of people on the earth this area was covered by a Precambrian Sea that produced *protocardia*.

Yet this relatively recent arrival of the human being has tracks in this area only in the *prehominids* period, our ancestral form that became the form that we are now. But humankind is not just an animal and we do not just unfold according to a "plan" that Nature set in motion. We are also Spirit manifesting through physical forms. Nonetheless, just as the physical evolution has proceeded through stages and left its tracks, so too has the evolution of our spiritual nature revealed itself in the history books and religious traditions that we find today.

In Acts 17, we read of a meeting the Apostle Paul had at the Areopagus, a "court-like" arena near the Acropolis in Athens. The Areopagus is an important "artifact" and place in the history of Western consciousness. The Areopagus was a place where the citizens met to discuss issues of the day and to make important decisions. What a step forward these Greek city states made in human togetherness! There are so many different ways we can organize ourselves into community – kings, tribal leaders, war leaders – but the Greeks had figured out democracy, a marvelous evolutionary experiment.

Our gathering here today has a great deal to do with what those Greeks initiated in the realm of human affairs and politics. Yet you can hear from Paul's discourse that he noticed that they were pretty traditional when it came to expressing their gods. They had a great reverence for gods, and they understood that there were authorities in the world that were bigger than human beings. So, they assigned various roles in the natural realm to various deities and personalities in the spiritual realm, which they called the Pantheon. All the qualities of the world, like wind and wisdom, were assigned personalities, and were propitiated or worshipped accordingly.

Lest we give the Greeks too much credit, this democracy only counted for the citizens who were members of the "in-group," slaves and women were not considered voting members of their fledgling experiment in human togetherness. So the apostle Paul, convinced to his core of what he believed, walked into the heart of the town where they gathered for discussion and said, "Listen, I have got some-thing to share with you. I have something that will blow you away. I can see you are religious people, and that you care about the subject I am going to offer you." Paul then proceeded to tell them that death has been overcome. I can imagine them saying, "O really! Aren't you interesting Paul!"

Right away Paul made himself irrelevant. These rational Greeks who had developed democracy were intelligent enough to know that when you die, you die. Yet here is a man witnessing to them that a human being was raised from the dead. Most of them blew him off. Some of them said that they would like to hear more another time. But they made him irrelevant in one way or another. They considered themselves superior and sophisticated to him. Keep in mind that they were the elite of the time.

Throughout history, there have been many ways to relate to the great mystery and ultimate Reality. Yet we are each left with very personal questions: "Where did we come from?" and "Where are we going?" We did our evolving biologically and politically through various social experi-ments, but evolution stops when it comes to humankind figuring out our own being and purpose in life. There is no way we are ever going to figure ourselves out on our own.

But God, in God's infinite mercy, compassion and capaci-ty has made Godself known to human beings in a way that is stunning and life-altering if only we have the ears to hear and bear it. And so it is that Jesus, in the Gospel of John, says to his disciples, "I am telling you the truth, and there is a lot more to tell, but you could not bear it right now. I could tell you more, but you could not bear it" (John 16.12).

I remember being a young man coming back to the Bible, being awakened and excited with the new discoveries in spirituality and religion, and reading that there was "more," but that we "could not bear it." I tried to visualize myself as a disciple: having seen people raised from the dead, having seen the sea calmed, lepers healed, the lame walk, the blind and deaf healed, and being told that "there was more," and "I could not bear it!"

However, Jesus said, "when I depart from you, I will send my Spirit of truth who will tell you everything you need to know" (John 14.26). Here we have, on the one hand, the progression of Athenian democracy and the intellectual thrust of Western thought trying to philosophically figure out the apostolic message. On the other hand, we have a man who knows where he is going, and that he cannot die. The Apostle Paul is witnessing to them about something that they did not yet get in full or understand rationally. While many Greeks accepted a concept of eternal life with judgment according to deeds, and others postulated that all who died went to Hades, or the underworld, it was the concept of a bodily resurrection to eternal bliss or communion with God, rather than the gloomy placidness of the Elysian Fields that would have been good news to them.

Thus, what Christ is saying through Paul is a new revelation. It is the revelation of the Holy Trinity. It is a most amazing revelation from God toward humankind that no human being ever figured out or will figure out. What the Trinity offers to us is not a theological point of view, or a dogmatic assertion, but an offering of relationship. Whereas the animists and pantheists see a cosmic ocean and living spirits moving everything, Christ has revealed to us the One God that is so One that this God can even talk to us and guide us individually and personally from within ourselves for everything we need to know. This God can reveal to us each personally that we will never die. This truth can be so convincing that no amount of intellectual scholarship could present you with enough arguments to sway your certainty.

The Trinity is the most amazing revelation of the intimacy of creation. It reveals how the universe is vast and cosmic, but it is also close and personal as a mother and a child. The revelation of God through Christ is the revelation of a Father who sent the Son to reveal to the entire human race that our identity is not finite or limited. We do not begin or end with the appearance or disappearance of the body. The Holy Spirit, our advocate, tells each of us everything we need to know. The Spirit is already in place within us, waiting for us to get tired of being like the Greeks trying to figure it all out; trying to get on top of the mystery; trying to get in control of it. None of us is in charge of anything. Every now and then when the earth shakes we are reminded of this. Every now and then when a great tidal wave comes we remember how tiny and vulnerable we are.

Yet sometimes when we send a Hubble Telescope into space and turn it back on the earth to perceive ourselves, we think we are a pretty big deal. Yet, we did it with the intelligence that was supplied to us by our loving creator who gives us keys to investigate the natural mysteries, teaching us how things fit together so that we can improve our lot in life and participate in the ongoing evolution of the human species.

This God at the same time brings us to a point of humility and smallness where we come before God with our helplessness and our great need for help. This God reveals to us personally and in each one of us that we are sons and daughters. That we are not left out in the cold and we are not at the whim of vast evolutionary forces. We are personally cared for by an intimately loving God who rescues us from ourselves when we call out for help and simply become small, going beyond our intellectually based figuring, counting and explaining. Divine help often happens when we are simply aware of our great need. This is the miracle moment the Advocate, the Spirit of truth, the Holy Spirit, shows up to tell us everything we need to know.

The Father is our Source. The Son is our form. The Holy Spirit is the intimate power that guides and leads creation forever and individual beings through all kinds of life situations, personally and in detail. These details are being led and guided by God. When we are listening, we can know it. There is nothing grandiose about the Holy Spirit. The Spirit is very quiet. The Spirit is a still, small voice within us. It takes some education for us to hear the Spirit. Maybe some de-education too. If fact, perhaps we have to first forget a lot of the ideas about control and being wonderful and figuring it all out.

Our Way-Shower, our Elder-Brother Jesus, showed us that the Way is love. Love is the way of going down into smallness, down toward the other person, down into the intimacy brought to us by our common vulnerability. O how much we need the help of God and each other in community to live a truly human Life. Anybody can fill up their head with words and knowledge. But it all comes to the moment when we are asked to put it down. When our time on earth is finished and we look back on our life, we might discover that it was not worth much. In contrast, our lives are written in love. The Lord showed us the way to love. It is not the way of trying to preserve one's self, but the way of giving it all away, guided by the Spirit, led by the Father in utter certitude into the depths of love, which is God.

The Trinity has always been intonated, just like the *proto-cardia* was the first attempt at the shape of a heart form. The Trinity is God's most complete revelation. The Hindus knew about the Trinity: Brahman. Vishnu. Shiva. The Vedas speak of it as Sat. Chit. Ananda. Intimations of the Trinity have always been around. Yet now in the Christian revelation of the Trinity, God is personal. It is almost unbelievably personal how much God loves each of us. How much God wants exactly a "you" and exactly a "me," and how much God treasures us as God's very own.

There is a price in knowing this sonship and daughtership. The price is turning toward home. Like the Prodigal Son, we finally get that becoming a philosopher is not going to do it. Being rich and knowing everything is not going to do it. What is required is turning and returning home back to the place where we started saying, "Father, forgive me. This is what I have done with the life you have given me. Here it is. I am now all yours." And the Father will say to us, "Let the party begin." No questions asked. Can we believe that? Can we believe that death is done? That sin has been utterly abolished and forgiven? The price of admission is to come toward God and find out if God means it. I think we will end that right there. Amen.[5]

∞

Six

Life in Love

∞

"They said to her, 'Woman, why are you weeping?' She said to them, 'They have taken away my Lord, and I do not know where they have laid him.'" John 20.13

What our senses seem to be reporting to us is not what an objective observer would see, if such a person existed. It is vital to know that in between the sensory report and the experience of our self, there is a whole train of logic and reason that acts as an intermediary shaping the mirror of the mind, reflecting something that actually is not there. This predicament intensifies around the age of seven years old, at which point our sense of mystery drops away and we start thinking and having problems. We start needing to put up a self that is over and against other selves.

The senses we rely on to know that this is a "this" and that is a "that," have at their base a flawed sense of perception called reason. Now reason is a wonderful tool. It is a beautiful tool for dealing with the world of objects and things and facts. It helps us deal with that which can be quantified, compared, weighed and balanced, but reason really takes in a small slice of what actually is. Since reason took over as the supreme human faculty in the era of the Enlightenment, the human condition has been in a state of decline.

However, the qualities of life, the experience of feeling the subtle shades of love and joy, peace and patience are not accounted for in reason. These qualities are *unreasonable*. Thus we have a truncated world we relate to through our screen of logic that only lets certain information in and filters the rest as irrelevant. Often, our senses have to do a bank shot off our logic in order to tell us anything.

Over time, the awe and wonder of childhood dissipates. On the one hand this is unfortunate, because it was in childhood that we could really see a blue sky. Or really smell the lilacs or freshly mown grass. All of these were numinous experiences in our childhood but through our absorption into rationality we slowly lose touch with the mystery of presence and subtle perception beyond the lock-down of rational logic in our thinking mind. On the other hand, we need to develop reason so to reach our full potential in life, but the problem is that we get stuck at the level of reason, fascinated with its power, forgetting that it too is just a step on the ever unfolding journey toward spiritual integration, and for that we need Spirit.

Spirit is the "something" in each of us that is longing for more than reason. The unconscious, the emotions and even the body itself all want to have a say; eventually they will reveal themselves to us, try as we may to repress them. They want to be free, and they return to our conscious experience sometimes in the strangest ways, especially in the experience of falling in love. When we are in love reason does not matter anymore. We suspend doubt and believe the unbelievable. We experience an opening of the heart. The mind opens up in love and everything seems different and more alive, at least for a little while.

We cannot stay in love without clearing out the screen of logic that has been accumulating the debris collected over our lifetime. So being "in love" is a state of reality. It is a truth that God has made us for. As the Song of Songs says, "O where is my lover!" (Song 7.12). This passage is the supreme example of the longing that patterns our union with God. St. John of the Cross wrote tremendous commentaries on the Song of Songs, and all the mystics have loved this Song because it describes the soul's longing for love beyond reason. We hear the heart's cry: "Where is my beloved? I have got to have my beloved!"

St. Paul speaks of this also when he says that "all of creation groans with inexpressible longings waiting for the sons and daughters of God to be born" (Romans 8.22). There is a love in us that wants to be born and we are squashing it with reason. It is not reasonable to feel so in love. It is not reasonable to have these God-longings that transcend the world. To long for something or someone you cannot see, touch, or that no scientist can prove with a formula or duplicate in an experiment is, through the lens of reason, utterly foolish. Yet that is just the kind of fools God is looking for. The wisdom of this world is foolishness to God. The wisdom of reasonableness and the wisdom of God which is love is utter insanity to the world, but inexplicable Life to those who have been touched by this unexplainable force of love.

We have as a model the "foolish" years of love we went through in our growing up years. We learned to have our hearts opened to the mystery of love. O how we did crazy things, but O the feeling! I will never forget the first time I ever kissed a girl. It was magic under a streetlight after a dance on a Saturday night by an alley next to her house. I can still see the ivy crawling up the telephone pole. I can still feel my heart beating and thinking, "O my God, we are going to, yes, we are kissing!" A door in my heart opened at that moment. I did not know a person could feel that way before that moment. All of a sudden there was a whole new realm of embodied life for me in Meadville, Pennsylvania. I did not know that kind of feeling was there before, because since I was a young kid I had been captured by reason and was trying to look like I knew what I was doing and fit in with the crowd.

The passion that awakened in me through that experience kept me thinking about that beautiful girl, whom will call Pat. Within two days she was holding hands with someone else at school and not talking to me. I found out what the opposite swing of the pendulum was. I was crushed. In love one moment, devastated the next. O the ache and longing inside. Do you remember that feeling? Do you remember the crying out: "Please, God, let it not be true!"

Do you know what I am talking about? Sure you do. The saints have been touched by God like that. Just like that. The longing is what makes them saints. It made them crazy. Totally dissatisfied with reason and logic and all the things you can count, have, hold onto and show off in this world. None of it meant a thing anymore in the embrace of irrational divine love. Now, another door opens in their being and they know the love of God and nothing will ever satisfy them again.

After I graduated from college I lived in Toronto. I can remember the very day I was kissed by God. I was sitting at my desk reading Alan Watt's book *The Wisdom of Insecurity.* As I read a description of why music is beautiful and why you kill the music if you hold on to each note, something happened in my mind, as though I could see my thoughts swivel on their axis 180 degrees, and I thought I have been seeing everything backwards! "O my God!" And a door opened in my heart. Suddenly the world looked different. I felt different and knew that my values were all upside down and I did not care anymore what anyone thought of me. It was the first time since high school that I was not comparing myself to others or what I thought was acceptable.

I was a shy person at the time. And I fell in love by the touch of God in my heart. I was in love with God and with everyone for three weeks. I started talking to strangers, picking up hitchhikers, talking to cleaning ladies, postal workers and elevator operators. I was in love with every one of them. I was in a new world. Yet it went away after three weeks. What I learned from the experience was that this was my first free kiss. Now, I had to find out how to make this love a permanent state in me. Like the Song of Solomon, I needed to go through the streets of my inner town and the rooms of my interior house saying, "Where is my beloved!"

Once the feeling comes to us there is nothing else that is as important to us. We know something now that transcends the physical world. We know the touch of the experience of God that is no longer dogma, doctrine or theology. It is an experience. And now we know when we have had this experience why the saints and martyrs acted so seemingly crazy. They were in love and they knew something. They were having an experience that transcends the world of logic reported by the senses. It is a love that enters into the domain that is usually repressed in people – the domain of the heart. It is there where we have eyes to see in another way.

This sight is the vision of the eyes of faith. We even begin to hear a different way. When the mystery opens up, we begin to see life in a totally different way. We become inexplicable to those around us just like we do when we fall in love. Touched by the transforming love of God, we no longer want to gossip. We no longer need to defend ourselves against being misunderstood. We discover that it is easier just to leave your heart open and be taken wrongly because the issue is no longer who is right or wrong, but rather how do I keep my heart open. How do I allow this heart to stay open so that the flood of love that is touching me inside will flow into my world, touching and kissing the people I look at and am in relationship with?

How can I see those I see and say, "There my love is in his or her distressing disguise." Can I see my lover, my beloved in stranger and friend alike? The Spirit of God can do this in each of us. The God of love who touches us from time to time wishes to remind us of what is true and enduring. Mary Magdalene shows us a good example of this. She was involved in historic events. She is a witness of history being split in half. Lightning struck the earth in the person of Jesus Christ and Mary Magdalene witnessed love coming into the physical earth standing on human feet showing us what love can do.

Mary saw this love. She saw this love raise the dead, the lame made to walk, the maimed healed, the deaf made to hear and the blind given sight. She heard stories of things that happened when she was not present in person. She even knew about Jesus walking on water. She knew about turning water into wine. She knew that for love itself nothing was impossible.

But at Jesus' tomb everything was shattered. She was in the Garden at the empty tomb. Her whole world had fallen apart. Her heart had been opened and she had been touched by this amazing love and now all of a sudden it was in tatters. And on top of that the traces of his presence were gone. She was distraught. I cannot even imagine it. I love Thomas Keating with a kind of love that I can scarcely even comprehend. I have loved my teachers. What they have brought me and what they have given to me. There is so much I did not know until they brought it to me. I love these people, and to imagine them suddenly taken away is more than heart rending.

Can you imagine Mary wanting to tear her garments and gnash her teeth saying "What have you done with my master!" So much so that she did not recognize the man standing in the garden as Jesus. She missed him yet he was right there. She was looking at something else. She was distraught by the empty tomb. She expected his body to be in there.

Then, Mary hears a voice speaking to her, but dismisses it as the gardeners', that is, until he says her name: "Mary!"

Thomas Keating has said that nobody could speak that name like Jesus could. Mary turned around and cried, "Teacher!" Mary's heart overflowed with the reality of his presence in her life. The first thing Mary did is the first thing we want to do when we come into love and what I tried to do with Pat. We want to hold onto it. I wanted to hold onto my experience in Toronto. I wanted to keep it mine forever and never let it go. Yet what are we asked? Jesus says to Mary, "Let go of me."

We know what the subsequent events were. She did let go and he continued to manifest his life to all kinds of people. Some of whom never even saw him as he was before his resurrection, like St. Paul. And yet Paul did see him and experience the risen Jesus Christ, speaking face to face in a non-corporeal exchange. A true dialog between two individuals happened between Christ and Paul. Although Christ was invisible to Paul's senses, Christ was absolutely real to Paul. So too is present in risen form in the heart of every single one of us today.

But, why you ask don't we see Christ? Perhaps our attention is looking somewhere else? Maybe our love is longing for someone else? We are spending our energy feeling forsaken and brokenhearted because it is not getting what it expected and it is missing the love that is always in our hearts saying our own names. It is saying our names with the very same ache that we feel for God, our ultimate reality.

We all know that something is really missing. We have been trying with our addictions and all our consumerism to fill this gaping wound that is calling for meaning and truth. We have tried every way we could to satisfy our longing but we did not realize that Christ is standing here all the time saying our own name. O how we are loved. And through this love doors open into realities that the senses have not dreamed of and logic cannot contain or even describe. So how do we find our lover?

The first thing we do is make ourselves available, because the soul is passive. It is receptive. The soul is not an active vehicle. It cannot go chasing. It has to open and long for the very thing that draws Christ in. Where are you my love? Where are you my beloved! The answer is unbelievable. All along, Christ is right here for Mary and right here for Paul and right here for us.

There is a seduction going on in the reports of the senses, as given by reason, telling us that we are separate from each other. They tell us that we are separate from God, that we are separate from safety, peace and good. That report is false. The lie of separation is *the* fundamental lie and the father of all the rest of the lies. If we can get that there is no separation, that this is Love's world and that Love wants us more than we want it, then we can let our lover pursue us.

Love is here. Our Lover is here. Perhaps we are just too busy. Or, perhaps we have not really yearned or longed. Perhaps we have not really allowed divine love to be a kind of information that is bigger than the promises of the world of things. One of the Psalms says it best, "My soul is longing for you, like a thirsty deer by a stream" (Psalm 42.1). The longing does the work, that is to say, it is the prerequisite, because when we are full and satisfied God cannot get to us. In our need and hunger for this divine love, God meets us experientially so that we do not have to wonder. We will not have to get into our heads about it and ask, "Was that actually a spiritual experience?"

That is what the head wants to do. It wants to tell everyone it had a spiritual experience too! Please remember that the experience is between you and God. It is very intimate, this heart business, very close and personal. The desire with which we desire God is God's desire for us. We have not even made our own desire. Love is a no brainer. And that is the problem. Amen.[6]

∞

Seven

Life at Center

∞

"The twenty-four elders fall before the one who is seated on the throne and worship the one who lives for ever and ever; they cast their crowns before the throne, singing..." Revelation 4.10

The rich and lavish imagery that John uses in the book of Revelation reveals layers of meaning. What jumps out to me is that we are getting a look into what John wants us to understand about the center of creation: at this center, there is a throne.

The throne image is useful for us to understand how authority comes down from the Creator to the created. It does not mean there is an actual big chair in the middle of heaven. It means that authority is vested in the center, and that from the center radiates an auric hue pouring out and passing through a zone of crystal and sea, surrounded by elders saying "Holy, Holy, Holy." In other words, emanations are pouring out of the center, and these emanations are reflected back by those who are nearest the center. Holiness is the name of the game at the center of creation. God is pouring forth holiness from the center and the twenty-four elders are reflecting it back.

At the periphery where we live in the Milky Way Galaxy, we do not see the center of our galaxy. It seems distant from us. Similarly, the creator does not seem to be present. We cannot see the spiritual center of reality with our physical eyes either, and so we have to take the witness of the saints and sages who have gone before us.

But that is not all. We can also test our own experience and see what we can find out about authority and centers. We know that if we look at the macrocosm, that is, the greater whole, it is in some way echoed in the microcosm, the particular.

Thus, each of our lives, in some way, is echoing the structures or organization that set up the whole universe. Centering Prayer is a spiritual practice that enables us to give our attention so to act like the twenty-four elders' attention, giving all the glory to the center and returning all the light and attention that is coming from the center back to the center itself.

Where is our center? It is the heart. Where the being of our life is resting; where the unseen is pouring into the seen; where eternity is pouring into time. Unlike the twenty-four elders who are elders because they know how to give their attention to the center, we have taken our attention, and instead of returning it to our Source, we direct it elsewhere.

We look at the periphery of things. We have looked at what in the East is called the names and forms, or the "The Ten Thousand Things." We have noticed the creation. We have liked things in the created realm, gathering and acquiring them, but we often ignore the presence of the creator in the created. Just as we often ignore our own hearts beating, we forget to notice God. Where is the instruction for the heart to beat? It is coming from the center of creation where all of life is pouring out from, and the authority of creation is manifesting itself and every possibility that may be.

All that we see in the created realm is simply a shadow or intimation of the presence that is at the center of creation. The master emanates light out into the world and if we are wise, we reflect that light back. If we recognize the Source, we might say something like: "Holy, Holy, Holy, is the Lord God. Glory to you, O Lord. I am not worthy to be healed, but since you are gracious and merciful God, I will give my whole being to you."

What the book of Revelation is teaching us is that there is a pattern to creation. It is echoed in the solar system, in cells and in human beings. Life moves from centers toward circumference and back again. The center re-gathers everything into itself, taking everything that has emanated in its oneness and loves it back into wholeness at the center.

Just as we sometimes see our own journeys leading us into a far country, taking our attention onto peripheral things that are of no consequence, when we come to ourselves and realize that we have been eating husks, we discover that the center has been waiting for us all along.

The Father, our Source, our Center, welcomes us with love. Our wandering attention returns to the Father with no penalty; no explanation is required. The Father embraces us and says, "Just happy to see you. Glad you are home." We are back to Life at the center. In the interval between our emanation, or our sowing into the world like seeds, and our return back into the heart of the Father, time occurs. History happens. Our story unfolds.

Eternity is where the Father is generating creation. Yet, such generation is outside of time. The same values don't hold inside time because here things are not eternally generated, they are decaying and passing away. Things rise up, persist for a while and then they decay. Like waves on the ocean they rise, persist and fall back into the water. Nothing is permanent here in the world of the Ten Thousand Things, in the world of Names and Forms.

What is permanent here is the Spirit – the Spirit that is running through the whole of creation and that animates us, bringing light to our minds, love to our hearts. The Eternal Spirit is right here manifesting the creation and animating it. This manifestation is here for us to notice, if we only have eyes that truly see.

This is important because when we look at the creation we get to see the creator. The creation did not happen by itself. It did not just become slime mold that got intelligent and then became the human brain. It did not just write a Bible, and then articulate abstract concepts about the center. John, the writer of the book of Revelation, wants us to know that the creator at the center has created and continues to create the creation.

Another dimension of the center is described in Jesus' parables: the ruler says "Did you not know that I am a jealous king?" Meaning, I want something back for everything I give. I am an efficient creator. There is a cause and effect. They are co-equivalent. There is a balance in everything in this creation. The Master does not just put something out there and not want it back.

Thus, in our human beingness we have been sown into life and God has endowed us with talents and gifts and qualities that each of us is accustomed to calling "our own." Yet we rarely notice our absolute dependence on our creator. When we are endowed with these qualities the Lord expects something to happen to them. The Lord expects them to be used, invested, enlarged and filled in. Just in case we misunderstand this principle, Jesus continues the parable saying, "To those who have, more shall be given. To those who have not, what little they have will be taken away" (Matthew 13.12).

What might this mean? To those that have more, more shall be given. To those who have none, or who squander that which they have, atrophy sets in. What little they have dries up and becomes unavailable.

Our personal will enters into the equation here, and if we are wise we will be like the twenty-four elders who are bowed down before the center of creation, bowed down before the throne praising the Source and the Author. If we are foolish we will hide the talent, keep it under a bushel, hold it as our own, and not use it for the common good or for the glory of the Creator. In the end, we will be called into account. There is always an accounting in this balanced universe. There is a justification or a justice that wants to happen.

Fortunately God is just, but as Thomas Keating is fond of saying, "God is not *just* just." There is mercy and compassion available. At the end of the game when all the players put their cards on the table and come back home, it is all free and clear for every single person even if we have invested our talents poorly, like I did in drunkenness.

All of it gets forgiven for the simple asking, "I want to come home, Father. I want to come back to the center and let my life be a glory to you." Even if it is in the last thirty seconds, or the very last second, any attention returned to the Father is truth. It came from the center. All that we call our own has come from God, and when, with understanding, we give it back to God the equation is complete. The dance of life goes on without anyone calling their own tune, but with all of us who have understood how it works dancing to the Lord's song, dancing to Life, glorifying and praising God, and serving our brothers and sisters who are likewise dependent on the center for everything, whether we know it or not.

The world does not welcome people who work only for the center. The world does not value the center. It values the circumference and the things that appear on the periphery. So, we are not going to be congratulated or supported very much for working for the Life at the center. But then, who cares about that? Who needs support from unprofitable servants when the twenty-four elders are encouraging us to live lives of truth and wholeness that say, "Holy, holy, holy Lord, God of power and might, heaven and earth are full of your glory – Hosanna in the highest – blessed is he who comes in the name of the Lord – Hosanna." Please observe yourself: have you been coming in your own name, or have we been coming in the name of the Lord?

This is a choice we make, minute by minute, second by second: Who do I work for? Who is my Lord? What is my center? Am I under my own authority? If so, I can get away with that for a while with my little three-score-and-ten on the surface of the planet, but when the cards are called, what will I say to my Author as the account of my life is revealed? "Here is what you gave me, Lord, and here is what I did with it." You would want to know because every second is a brand new second to choose again. Every day is a brand new day to start over. The eternal part of life is always here and always fresh and new. The temporal part of life is passing away. The center is ours to return to again and again if only we will. Amen.[7]

∞

Part Two:

The Contemplative Year

∞

Eight

Advent

∞

"As it is written in the book of the words of the prophet Isaiah, the voice of one crying out in the wilderness: 'Prepare the way of the Lord, make his paths straight.'" Luke 3.4

What would it take to experience the spiritual aspects of Christmas? How can we create a Christmas season less consumed with commercial consumption and more concerned with participation in the incarnation of Light, Life and Love? That is why we are here. Humanity is here to discover who we are, to discover what God is, and to transcend the small identities that seem to define and limit us. The Christmas season is the discovery of the Truth of who we are as the human race.

Jesus Christ, born in the stable two thousand years ago was the historical equivalent of a small comet striking the earth, the shock waves of which are still penetrating human experience. This event invites each of us to that historical, yet also close and personal experience of Christ in me and Christ in you. While the obscuring factors of commerce and economics can limit our Christmas experience, the Light of God's presence is available to us in Christ so to rediscover the ancient potency and grace made visible in the birth of Jesus for the new-birth of humanity.

In Christ we are free to enter the world of commerce and culture. As Jesus prayed for his disciples in the Gospel of John, we are to be "in the world, but not of it" (John 17). Our identity in Christ enables our participation in the world – fearless and free, loving and generous – because we know that our good comes from God, not from any condition or station in life.

While our culture thrives on the ongoing fragmentation of the identity of the human being, our aim in this season of Advent is to become unified, knowing who we are in every area of our life, our marriages, work and our relationship to money. Using the spiritual tools of Centering Prayer and Work ideas, we can become unified and balanced human beings. These spiritual tools enable us to deal with our inner reality, which is our consciousness.

Life is the way it is externally because of our inner being. The reason our external circumstances are like the way they are is because our internal consciousness is the way it is. When we have confusion in the outer world it is merely mirroring the confusion in the inner world. This in sum is what the Work terms, "Your being draws your life." If you would like to change the circumstances of your life, change your being. This change of being is uncanny because it always brings a deepening growth in order, balance and supply in our life circumstances.

One tool we can use regarding supply is the pamphlet *"Solving the Problem of Supply"* by W. Frederick Keillor. In this pamphlet, Keillor teaches principles of understanding that will allow us to be in a right relationship with our Source so that our needs manifest automatically without fear, and in a balanced way. Our supply meets our demand because we have understood how to place ourselves in relationship to our Source. *"Solving the Problem of Supply"* is a recipe, and if you want the "soup" that this recipe offers, you have to cook by the recipe, which will require mental discipline; disciplines which encourage lightness of touch and freedom of thought. Yet, the recipe does not include worry or concern. Why?

Because our minds are always manifesting, and if we are always thinking "not enough," the world has no choice but to return an image of not enough. But when we understand that we belong to God and that our supply is God's business and live that way, we will always have enough. Knowing this, to feel concerned about our supply would be as silly as a cell in your body wondering if it will get enough blood. This is God's business. Just as that cell is the body's business, we in Christ are God's business. In Christ, we are cells in God's living, spiritual body.

Yet, we are free to isolate ourselves and turn away from God. We are free to contain ourselves in our own self-bound strategies, which ultimately are self-defeating every time. Solving the problem of supply by using the spiritual tools of Centering Prayer and Work ideas will set any life right in every dimension.

This is true because at the deepest part of our humanity, the core of our being is the living One. Christ is the single identity of all identities. The Christ that is the manifestor and constant presence in all creation is waiting to be discovered by our attention. Thus, our ontological identity never changes. We have always been what we are now and we will always be that. Yet the truth of our experience of being united with Christ has to come through an educated process of discerning and noticing when we are identified with our roles and relationships that we play in life. Behind all our roles, experiences, thinking, feeling and doing is the living One, and there is no other.

During the Advent season we begin to realize that what was born in Bethlehem was indeed an individual human being. Moreover, this specific human being embodied the general human nature of all of us. The recognition of him in Palestine two thousand years ago is incomplete until it includes the recognition of that birth going on as the continuation of the Light in and through us.

Consciousness is light. Unconsciousness is darkness. As the Christmas carol reminds us, "Long lay the world, in sin and error pining." That is, the world remains in darkness; the beings of the world do not know who they are.

As the Light has gradually dawned, generations of people have caught on, and experienced that this Christ-birth is in them too! The dawning of the Light acted out on the stage of history in the characters of the biblical drama can also go on in me! The Virgin Birth is here in my soul saying, "Lord how can this be, but let it be in me according to thy word" (Luke 1.38).

Here in these darkest days of winter, when we feel most separate, alienated and in doubt, the answer to the cry of a hungry world is being born in each of our hearts. The willingness of each of us to be the mysterious vehicle for that continuing birth is the answer. Our willingness to follow Mary in the mystery of vulnerability, saying Yes to God is the heart of Christmas. We are manifestations of Christ. Just as every acorn is an oak tree in its acorn phase, so too is the birth of Christ the flowering of humanity, available to each of us if we apply the living water of the Spirit through spiritual practice. The acorn and the tree are one thing in two phases.

The birth of Christ in us will occur just as an acorn will become an oak tree when the conditions are right. For humans, we can set our conditions. We can give our time and awareness. We go where we look. Our lives follow our attention. To attend to these inner, living things is the invitation of the Spirit in this Advent season. There is a living mystery going on and it wants to include you and me.

At Christmastime, we do not have to be wonderful. We are just grateful to be alive, happy that our little shells are splitting open and that the Light of Christ is beginning to break out through us and shine on the world around us. Through this process, we are liberated from judgment, fear and doubt, and most of all, from our self-bound identities stuck in their cultural conditions thinking that the way of the world is the only way to happiness.

Let us open to the mystery of Christ this Advent and discover again what the Way to abundant Life is. Amen.[8]

∞

Nine

A Conscious Christmas

∞

"But the angel said to him, 'Do not be afraid, Zechariah, for your prayer has been heard. Your wife Elizabeth will bear you a son, and you will name him John.'" John 1.13

John the Baptist is the last of the prophets of Israel. At the time of John's arrival, Israel's prophetic tradition had been happening for at least two millennia. But why the need for prophecy in the first place? And why the need for a messiah? The answer that compels me at Christmas is that it comes right down to noticing the human condition in its manifold forms of our dance of alienation. It is that very alienation that called forth the prophets and the messiah from the heart of a God who loves us. God is about closeness, not alienation.

In order to better understand the remedy of closeness and oneness, let us explore the sickness and alienation. Our human condition has been variously described as a condition of "sin" which really means "missing the mark," or even "missing the point." Sin is a condition of our fallen human nature, which means that humankind continues to live out of touch with reality.

Some speak of it as an un-evolved nature. However we define it, the truth remains substantially the same: *something is not right here*. We are not living in the way we were intended to by our creator. We were meant for so much more than war, so much more than the use of technology in unconscious ways and so much more than overconsumption. Something is not right about how we are living in relationship with each other and the earth. We have consumed to the point that our planetary home is on the verge of system failure. At a certain point we ask, "Why? What is going on here?" At that point it is tempting to enter into a consensus trance saying, "Well, there is a war and sure the poor are not fed, but that is just the way it is. Sure there is destruction of our planetary home, but we have to drill, mine and log to get our oil, gold, iron and wood."

It is just these kinds of moments of vulnerability the voice of the prophet appears on the stage of history to call humankind back to reality. Or, at least to call those who have ears to hear, who have eyes to look around and ask "What is going on here? How are you choosing to live?"

When I was a little kid I remember asking, "Why is there war, Dad? Why don't people just be nice to each other? Why don't they just get along?" It seems so obvious, but this is our condition: we are fallen from reality. We have descended into a vibrational frequency in which we are not in touch with the Source from which we have been and are being created, second-by-second. But God has always been calling God's people back to the Truth, back to the reality that, "I created you in my image and my likeness, and you were made for more than this."

Now, whenever a prophet accepted the call to become the voice of God in history, s/he also accepted the call to become alienated from their friends. Nobody likes the call of the prophet. It sounds like this: Repent! Turn around. Change your mind for God's sake! Change the things you are thinking about, the things you are engaged in, the things you treasure that are not worthy of children of God.

You have given away your divine birthright in favor of pleasures and self-satisfaction. Of course no one wants to be disturbed in their sleep. As a result, the prophets have been stoned and sawed in half. Over the centuries there were many ways of disposing of those prophets motivated by a desire to quiet that disruptive voice, a voice that disturbs our self-absorbed slumber and feeling that everything is just okay.

Today we have come to a time in human history when the "not-okay-ness" of it has caught up with us. There is now little room to continue our idiocy and sense of separation from God, one another and the planet. Thus through the prophets we are being called again to notice the truth. When John the Baptist announces that our redemption is near at hand, what does "near at hand" mean? It means *here*. It means *now*. It is not in some far-off heaven.

The trick is liberating our attention. Liberating it from the things our culture holds dear, which are the seeming necessities of acquisition and cultural displays of authority and power. We get hooked into them because we are products of the culture and are therefore imprinted by it. We are the inheritors of thousands of years of culture, all of which were based on the mistaken notion that we were separate from God and from each other. The result of this mirage is that we think things like, "I am in competition with you for scarce resources." We think there is not enough to go around. On and on it goes.

Now, it can be different for those who hear the voice and listen. For those who have ears to hear and do turn around; for those who do begin to change their thinking. This is why we need the prophets. During the Christmas season we hear announced in the scriptures, "Here comes the light! Pay attention!" Yet our culture has diluted the profundity of the message into "rock-a-bye Jesus in a manger." It is all very soft and cute. But listen to what the prophets are saying and you will hear it echo throughout the scriptures and down into the book of Revelation where the Spirit says, "Buy fine gold, immutable gold, from me, tried in the fire, tested, refined in the fire" (Revelation 3.18). So the prophets say, "Yes, He is coming. But who will endure the day of His coming? Who can stand when He appears for He is like a refiner's fire? He will sit purifying silver, and He will purify the sons of Levi refining them like gold or silver that they may offer due sacrifice to the Lord."

Now think of our planet Earth, hanging with our little moon anchoring the tides, orbiting the sun which makes everything grow. Yes, we have a blazing sun at the heart of our little part of creation! Yet is the creator of the sun brighter and more energetic than the sun? Yes! So of course God must have inherently more light and energy than the sun. Remember too that the sun is one of billions and billions of suns, and a minor one at that. Yes, the creator cannot be less than what was created, which means there is a lot of stepping down by the time life gets to us so that we can bear it.

For example, if we get out into the bright sun even now we get hot really fast, and if we stay out too long we are crisped. What this analogy is telling us is that the light of God's love is so pure, so vast and unimaginably great we cannot stand it. When we begin to turn to love and its brightness, and its unmediated presence everything in us that is less than that brightness, that is less than love crackles in the light and heat of the refiner's fiery love.

Now you can see this power from time to time when you get a dose of love and cringe from it. When we are faced with intimacy with our partners, sometimes we get real close and we feel our self pull back because we cannot take that much love. That is the stepped-down version between partners. When Christ came to Earth, when the creator God walked this earth, the Christ had to stop being as bright as the galaxy. The Christ had to stop being as bright as the sun. God stepped down to the presence that was held in Mary's womb. Remember, this is the author of creation and the Source of the stars. It steps itself down so we can come face-to-face with God and realize who we are because that is what Christ came to restore. The Christ came to restore the identity of a people who had turned away to seek their good when in fact that good was blazing in their heart the whole time.

We are told in scripture that we were created in the image and likeness of God. We have a form, or *image*, and then we have a spiritual presence, or *likeness*. Both of these are ours individually. Now the physical form we have never lost when we fell. That form will be with us through the worst and through the best. If we were in hell that form would be there. In fact, that is what can go to hell. The form is immutable, yet transformable. It is an eternal gift from God. But the *likeness*, that is what we no longer possess. It is the likeness of God that we desperately need restored in us. God is love. It is love that holds the atoms together. Love keeps our bodies in one place. It is love that keeps it all together, and then it holds all things together within the greater whole. It is love, and that love is hot stuff. So for us to return to the likeness of God requires us to use our will, because that is something God cannot violate.

God has given us the eternal form, but the likeness is up to us to request, cultivate and keep. Will we live like our creator in endless generosity? Will we give ourselves away? Will we share the light of the love within us, giving it away? As the sun gives its gift to all who walk on the earth no matter how they act, no matter how they feel, no matter what they do, so too will we live this way of giving? The call to us from the prophets at Christmas is to become the Light of the world. This is what the Christmas season is about. The Light stepped itself down from its holy place, and it took on the form of a human. Will you and I dare to become so fully human, incarnate so fully in these lives and bodies that we begin to take on the likeness of God again? Our will can be given to the great "Yes" of life instead of our resistant "No! No I do not like this. I do not like that." Thankfully our father is endlessly merciful, generous, gracious and kind.

Christ came to restore our original likeness that was created by God. With repentance we turn our minds around. It is a total regeneration. Jesus said "Follow me in the regeneration of your likeness to God. Now if we are to be regenerated, that is an affair of the heart and that regeneration happens through the refiner's fire, through the cross. Because we go to the cross to follow Christ into the redeemed situation of humankind we are lifted up, not by avoiding the cross and the difficulty of it, but by going straight through it following Christ through the resurrection and ascension back to the original heavenly estate in which the image and likeness are intact and restored. There we realize and live as one with Abba and all other beings. So the lie of separation is the original lie that the snake (if you want to use that image) whispered to Eve, "You are separate from God. You have a separate will. You can do your own thing. You can do anything you want. You will not die." O yeah, we died. We died to the likeness. When we took our will and made it our own, that very Luciferic pride, "I have got it. I will take it from here on. I am my own master now." That is the very thing that killed the likeness of God in us.

Separation is a total lie because we belong to God like cells belong to our own bodies. We are imbedded in God's being and in divine love. If we think we have lost it, grace can give it back. But it does not come like an abstraction where God takes the divine hankie and says, "O there, there. All better now?" The fire is the pain of letting go of our false identities, letting go of our neediness, our self-righteousness, our sense of having to lord it over others, of knowing what is best, of judgment, of criticism, of all the stuff that the poisonous heart is filled with so that the heart might be returned to the likeness of God and to endless generosity and love.

The pain of letting go of our old identities is the refiner's fire. It is not just, "Well there, I am going to let it go. I am going to turn my life to God and it will all be cool." That is easy to say, but we have to confront our unconscious inheritance from the generations of humanity that have gone before us. It is not just others, it is us, we are the people, and we are humanity in its personal and local form. And the healing of the species, of our regeneration, happens as individuals catch on to what the voices of the prophets were calling humankind to. The Incarnation of Jesus the Christ has made it possible. The repentance, the turning around, the regeneration, the changing of the heart, the redemption, the lifting up of the entire human race is now available for each of us. It happens molecule by molecule through our union with Christ.

The heat of this Lord is not an abstraction. It is a hot business to accept that Christ carried the sins of humanity, indeed our own fallen nature. We have just got to sink down and own it. We must see and confess, "O my God, I am just like all the people I do not like. I am just exactly like the people in government I am so fond of feeling better than. I am just the human race in person. O my God, I need help. I need help!" And God will say, "I was waiting for you to ask." God is the good shepherd. God has been looking for us the whole time, but we have been too busy to be found. God is ready to lift us up and to assist us by giving us the willingness to bear the unpleasant business of owning our own unconsciousness and say "Yes" to being healed of the lie of separation.

God is with us to give us strength. God is with us to help our faith. God is with us to give us insight and spiritual direction. Everything is available to us except our realization that we have a deformed likeness that we are not like God anymore. Yet we can be.

The way we currently are as a species on this planet is below the design specs. We are not living like human beings. We are living even worse than animals, because at least animals do not have a choice. We have choices, but we have given them away. We have given our will to cultural conditioning. We believe we have to behave and look a certain way so we will be esteemed. We may be esteemed but we are spiritually dead if we do not have the likeness of God within us. The joy of living a life that is generous, that is kind and loving, as described by 1st Corinthians 13. That is the likeness God wants to restore in us if we will follow Jesus into the Incarnation where there awaits for us a beautiful regeneration. So can we bear that heat? We were designed to. We were designed to be born again. Everything is in place except our willingness and our attention. Now it sometimes seems like we cannot handle it when we get into this. We probably had no idea what we were getting into when we got in the ring with God. And thank God we did not or we would not do it. But we are being called to die now. Can we do it? If you think you cannot, *will* it.

I have had the privilege of being at the birth of several human beings. There comes a point in the birth process where women say, "I cannot take it. This cannot be happening! It feels crazy!" But, please remember that a woman in travail, a woman giving birth suffers much, but she also has great joy because she knows something new is being born. When you and I get into this kind of relation-ship with God where we feel ourselves being spiritually called, where we feel the angelic help that is at hand, we understand that we are being born again and that God knows how to accomplish this work even if we do not. God has handled billions of these. God knows how to take an acorn out of an oak tree, and a chicken out of an egg, and a baby out of a human mother, and God knows how to get us to the next stage of spiritual Life too.

Do you want to? The truth is that each one of us is going to let go of this realm of forms at the point of death. At that moment we will let go of all the things we consider absolutely essential to our present estate. So why would we bother to wait until our moment of physical death to be spiritually reborn? The earth is groaning for this new Life. The human species is groaning to take God's offer up. Regeneration occurs not because we are wonderful, but because we are not. Only God is wonderful. We have the privilege of being called. It is a grace to be offered an entrance into the kingdom that is near at hand. There is nothing on the earth that can compare to this.

So here is the Christmas season, and here is the nativity waiting to happen in you and me. It is incubating like a slow fire now, but as the Light becomes more and more profound it will blaze up in us. That blazing Light will crisp everything else in us that is inauthentic and unreal. It will count us among the reborn; the twice-born that walk this earth like women and men were meant to walk. We will take our part among the people who were chosen to become fully human rather than products of culture. Products of culture are a-dime-a-dozen and you know where they go. Poof! As if they never were. None of our stuff goes with us.

This is the time of spiritual birth. This is the time of listening with an ear to the silent interior where God is always speaking and God's Word is near at hand. These are sacred moments of time and space, cosmos and creation where God is just waiting for someone to listen. The time of the prophets is over. They have said everything they can. Now is the time for the birth of the Son of God in this our human family, in you and me, and in all who will listen and consent. Amen.[9]

∞

Ten

Christmas Eve

∞

"In the beginning was the Word, and the Word was with God, and the Word was God. He was in the beginning with God." John 1.1

Tonight we share three Christmas stories: First, the story of Christ's coming in history in Bethlehem. Second, the cosmic story of the Eternal pre-existent Word. Third, the story of Christ's personal birth in each of us. The historical scenario is a story we are all familiar with. It is the story of Joseph, Mary and the baby Jesus born in a manger in Bethlehem, with angels, shepherds and wise men from the East.

The prologue to the Gospel of John provides an idea we may not have connected with the Christmas event before, especially as it is told from the perspective of the other three gospels. Uniquely, in the Gospel of John we see that Jesus is the Light coming into the world.

We have heard about his coming in history in Bethlehem, and we have heard about the cosmic reality of the Word made flesh, yet there is still something more. Thomas Keating offers us an opportunity to see further into the contemplative meaning and mechanisms of Christ's coming in each of us. Christ's birth is not complete until it is manifested in the hearts and minds of all the individual human beings in the world.

Thomas says that, "The feast of Christmas is the celebration of divine Light." The Son of God loves pure Light. The Son of God is pure Light. That Light is manifesting in each of us at every microsecond of our lives. It is the Light of love that is in our hearts.

Here on the table before us is the continuation of Christ's presence in history. We heard in the Christmas proclamation how history was split in half by God's incarnational presence in Jesus. Here in the Eucharist is the opportunity for each of our histories to split for a moment into the eternal Now, to have our past and our future interrupted by the living spiritual presence of the Living One in our hearts.

The Eucharist is the song of all creation coming back together in a single hymn of praise and thanksgiving. Here on the table is the summary of all of life in a host, carrying Spirit just like each of our bodies is a host for the Spirit. But this particular host is animated by the living intention of the historical Christ, saying, "This is my body." Christ is making a personal claim on all material creation and is inviting us to come back home to divine love.

In the cup is salvation and forgiveness; the forgiveness for all our human foolishness and folly, for the lives that we have lived because we thought we were separate from God and separate from each other. The Eucharist is the invitation to come back together, to come into God's great heart of love, to realize the Light that is the Life in all of us, and to participate in the ongoing incarnation of that Light.

The individual appearance of our lives sometimes makes us seem separate from each other. The Life that is in us is one Life. The humanity that we are is one humanity, and the Light which we know and by which we love is one Light, just as all these flames seem like separate flames, but it is only one fire. It is one conversion of matter into spirit and it is the very same thing that goes on in us. We are one Life together.

We celebrate the Incarnation of the Light and the Incarnation of Truth at this time of great darkness when the sun is at its lowest arc. Nevertheless, this is exactly the time when we can receive the Light that comes into the world to lift us above the gloomy spirit of news and culture. This is the season to realize the eternal realities that unify us, that make us one, and that bring us to the livingness that is eternal, and that transcends time and space in all conditions so to unify us into one single Life that lives us.

As we go from this place we will be lighting candles together, and we will see individual flames shared from one to the other as we go down the rows and pass the flame along. This is the very same process by which Christ has arrived to us, by which Christianity has come, by which the Eucharist has arrived. Jesus told Peter and Paul, and then they told others, and they told others, and they told others that the Light had come into the world, and now we can tell too.

How did we know it? Was it just words? No. It was by the Light in the faces of those who bore witness to the Light of Christ. It is by the Light of Life and Love in those who understand that they are called to live free of fear, and free to live in peace because joy has come into the world.

The Light of Christ is waiting for us to accept it just as we accept this flame from the person next to us. As the flame passes from me to Barbara to each of the ushers who will then deliver it to each row so to be accepted and then shared along down the row, we will see this room becoming lighter and lighter.

The fullness of Life comes when enough people get it. With this candlelight service we celebrate the possibility of doing our part, to bear and receive the Light, to pass it along for the joy of participation for the fullness of being because God made it possible.

As we exit the sanctuary row by row, let us do so in this amazing silence, and feel that presence from which our lives are emerging at every second, and feel the Spirit that wants to communicate itself to a hungry world through us. Amen.[10]

∞

Eleven

Ash Wednesday

∞

"Have mercy on me, O God, according to your steadfast love; according to your abundant mercy..." Psalm 51.1

I am in awe of the beautiful and humble hearts of monks I have met in monasteries all around the world. Meeting these monks has been one of my life's greatest privileges. I feel this way because when you see a genuinely humble person it is very attractive. Perhaps it is so attractive because it is so unusual.

When we are filled with ourselves and the affections that culture imprints on us and teaches us to value, there is a certain diminishment of presence, a certain inward turning of the attention to "self," and the loss of certain radiances that naturally communicates to hearts that are open to God. Humble hearts are not common. They are not ordinary in our culture and they are not ordinary today. Fortunately we have probably been touched by one, and have some taste of how attractive it is to be around a person who is not filled with themselves, nor filled with their own excellence, or, conversely, the subtle pride of unworthiness. Either way non-humility is a heart filled with the false self.

The 51st Psalm says, "A heart contrite and humble, O Lord, you will not spurn." So why do we want to have contrite hearts? Is it to be attractive to others? No. It is to be attractive to the Spirit and presence of God. Often, we try to fill ourselves with things that promise to fill our existential hunger and angst. But nothing ever fills it, because it is the Spirit of God that we were made by, for and in the image of its Truth and Reality.

In a culture that does not prize God there are no real human beings. There are only imitations of human beings. While there may be many human being seeds, like acorns, there are precious few oak trees for us to emulate. What will we do for models? While we may not have any positive models, we have a lot of models of what not to do and what not to be. Such models show us our culture does not work. Things just do not work here. They also did not work in other times and in other places because the world, absent God's presence, is a woeful and misbegotten place. It is not our home. When we have the world's values filling our hearts, we are not real people. We are in a world of shadowy people with shadowy presences, living out lives without meaning and wondering where the meaning is. But life is not hopeless. We know this because we have been given signs given from time to time from higher realities.

The point is that things do not work right when people forget God. Because we are capable of living in denial of Truth and God, hoping somehow that tomorrow will be different or that things will change magically, we fail to notice that they are not working. We live instead on false dreams imagining that somehow Tinkerbell is going to come and sprinkle fairy-dust on the whole occasion and make it turn out great. But because we live in a lawful universe things do not turn out great unless hearts turn toward God.

This lawful creation grows in power and manifests the things we give our affections to. If we give our attention to possessions and power, these things may certainly grow and get bigger, but we will ultimately be disappointed. In this world of opposites and duality, the law of the pendulum is unrelenting: the opposite is going to come. When we are always trying to stay on top, we will experience the bottom. If we always want to be right, we will be wrong. Our affections, when locked on to the world of things, will return to us unexpected sorrows. Pride is always brought low and the sense of the exalted self soon dissipates its energy source. At the end of our three-score-and-ten, we experience what is referred to as the final judgment, the cards are called. There we will be with the sum of what we have given our affection and attention to. Will it be counted worthy? Thus it is essential to return to the Source of our being.

To transcend and get out from under the law of cause and effect, or the Old Testament Law, an eye for an eye, a tooth for a tooth, as you sow so shall you reap, requires the power and presence of God and God's mercy. To attract God into our hearts we have to empty them of what they are full of now and humble them in contrition.

Contrition is a word we are not used to. We may say, "I am sorry I did that," but from what I have read of the accounts of people who have died and then returned, who have gone through the life-review process with the Being of Light, is that there in the presence of Love one does not think or say, "I should not have done that." Instead one feels the consequences that were visited on all the other beings who were involved in your life by your actions. We are not operating in a vacuum although we regularly act like we are. To be liberated from the karmic consequences of our love of things and pride, contrition is a wonderful exercise. It is the experience of noticing not only what we did or what we had affections for, but also feeling the abjectness of giving our hearts to things that ultimately leave us unsatisfied. How awful to live a life that was made for God, made for love, made to bear God's image into the world, when in fact all that time was spent puffing oneself up and chasing after the mirage of happiness in all the wrong places. There is a feeling that goes with such an inner awareness, it is scathingly self-honest and requires inner insincerity to admit how much we waste our lives in pride and self-love.

I remember the first time I felt true contrition. I was 29 years old. I was drunk. I went into the bathroom and looked in the mirror and there was this sad man who only thought of himself and whose life had become miserable because of his self-absorption and his attempts to constantly please himself. I remember saying then, "O God, you gave me a life and *this* is what I did with it." In that instant, I was truly sorry. It was not long after that moment of honesty that I desperately called out for help. God then filled my heart and I remembered what forgiveness was all about, because I really needed forgiveness.

It is not that we are awful people, or that we are evil, or that we are intentionally going out and doing bad things to people. It is that our hearts have been given to things that are not worthy of a human being. In contrition, we notice and hold the truth up to God saying, "This is what I have done with the life you gave me." When we become the humble heart that is attractive to God, God will not spurn it. When God fills that heart with Godself, we will be astounded to see how a human being can feel. When a human being is integral and authentic, true to her or his own deepest nature, it brings great joy. God has graces for us that are unimaginable in the worldly context. God is on another level, it is completely off our cultural maps. When the Spirit fills us with real life we wonder, "Why did I ever wait so long to give myself back to God?"

In the gospel reading for today, Jesus says you are looking for a sign, asking, "Is it safe to let go into you, Lord? Will you really take care of me? Show me." Jesus responds, "The signs have already been given." Jonah prophesied to the Ninevites and they gave it up. They understood that there would be consequences for their actions and that everything eventually comes to a place where the cards are called, where the game is up and we cannot do it our way anymore. At those moments we see our absolute dependency on God and that we have to own our choices.

Jesus says, "The Ninevites listened to Jonah and they repented. Likewise you will be judged." Not like a judge with a gavel, but compared to those who did listen, what did you do? They are a witness in the Bible. Did you believe their account of things and follow their example? Or, as with the Queen of Sheba with all her gold and riches and the opulence of her court, she heard there was true wisdom on this earth and she put everything aside to go in search of that wisdom. Now there is an example you can follow.

Jesus ultimately says that the only sign to be given is the sign of Jonah, the sign of going three days into the belly of the beast and then emerging with another life. He is also referring to the sign that he himself will be going into the earth for three days after his crucifixion, and rising from the grave completely and utterly alive in a brand new and almost unrecognizable way to those he knew before, revealing to us the infinite Life that is the capital "L" Life of our lives.

Jesus is telling us that his risen presence is within us now. The Life of Christ is in us now and that is our sign: the mystery of our own appearance; the mystery of our persistence and capacities. These mysteries are Life's aliveness in us. There is no private life. There is no "my" life and "your" life. There is the Life which is Christ's risen presence within us.

If we need more of a sign than that, before we let go of this pitiful thing we call "our life," with its petty affections and small attempts to protect itself, we will be there at the end of our days wondering, "Why did I wait so long before I caught on that I was not in control, or that I wasn't in charge of things? Why didn't I see that I am an absolutely dependent, utterly contingent creature, somehow maintained by the mystery of Life. Why did I live as if it was mine to do as I privately wanted, or to exclusively give my affections to temporal things that will only go away in the end?"

As we get older (and some of you may already be experiencing this) time seems to be accelerating. When I look back on the days now that were so long when I was young, well, they are gone. There is nothing left of them.

What is left of my prior experiences? What is left is the state of my heart. Is it full of vanity? Or is it humble enough and contrite enough for God not to spurn it but rather fill it? Only God and I know that. Nobody else can tell if my heart is filled with God. But here is a clue to use if we ever wonder if our hearts are filled with God: scripture tells us that, "Out of the fullness of the heart, the mouth speaks" (Matthew 12.34).

If our hearts are filled with God's presence, if they are touched by the Spirit, then we will be praising and blessing and healing the wounds of creation with our speech. We will be drenched with kindness, with a blessing that enlarges, empowers, encourages and uplifts. As we listen to our own speech about how awful things are, our dislikes, our judgments of others, we should be absolutely alarmed. There will be a price to pay for what we say. Nobody is going to do anything to us; we are doing it to ourselves. If our hearts are not filled with God it is not God's fault. God has given us many signs. God has made every possible way available for us to return. The only thing lacking is our attention, willingness and giving our will back to God.

Lent is the time to rediscover that there is no profit in the affection of worldly things. There is no profit of being seen by others to be this way or that way. We may remember that the people's tongues welcomed Jesus into Jerusalem saying, "Hosanna, hosanna, hallelujah!" Three days later the same voices cried out "crucify him!" There is no stability, there is no security, and there is no profit in the things we normally attend to. There is one thing alone that has any value eternally and that is our affection for the God who beats our hearts, brings Light to our minds, breaths us and shepherds us like sheep when we give ourselves back.

We worry asking, "Give me a sign that I will be safe, Lord. Give me a sign that you really will take care of me. Then I will let go." But open your eyes, look around, see what happens when you do not let go. Jesus says, "I am the good shepherd. My sheep know my voice." Are we listening to it? What an amazing image is this! Sheep are helpless, and they are not all that smart. They are looking at the ground all the time; they are not made to look up. But the shepherd wants them to be safe. He wants to protect them. He wants to guide them and guard them. He has an interest in them. The shepherd wants to take care of those sheep.

If we can be humbled enough to bring our pride down, enough to realize we do need to be taken care of and we do need to be shepherded through this realm of the wolves of cultural sense and possibilities, then the Good Shepherd will take us home to His own heart. There, we will be fed and taught. There, God will reveal to us the things we need to know to live the lives we were meant to live, the eternal lives that are here even now. Eternity is here. The risen Christ is here. God is not distant from us. It is our attention that is distant from God.

During Lent we open our eyes and our ears to our real need and we give up the distracted lie that everything is just okay. But, left on our own, it will not turn out okay. Every one of our efforts to take care of ourselves is flawed because it is based on the idea that we are separate from God, the Good Shepherd. Every one of our efforts has affection for the wrong things in it and as a result will give us things we are not intending. Unfortunately, things we do not want come with the things we try to get. The only way out is God's love, which has already been given. The sign is complete, thorough and total. Here is a witness to it as we look upon the communion table. God has invited us to come home to our own hearts, to humble ourselves enough to make room for God there, to remember that we have always been God's sons and daughters, and that God knows how to take care of us. "A humble and contrite heart, O Lord, you will not spurn." These are beautiful words to begin Lent on this Ash Wednesday. Amen."

∞

Twelve

The Lenten Journey

∞

"Yet even now, says the LORD, return to me with all your heart, with fasting, with weeping, and with mourning..."
Joel 2.12

"Be merciful to us Lord for we have sinned." The word "sin" has more capacity to be transformed than any other word we use in Christianity. Understanding the concept of sin has great leverage for us and our transformative process. So let us see if we can redeem that word for ourselves. Let us work to see it in the light in which it was intended, and offer ourselves a visual way of relating to it that allows us to get some leverage on it so that we can see the quality of sin in our self and offer it up to God for help.

Sin has a lot to do with ideas of "within" and "without." Keep in mind that our sense-based and evidence-based worldviews are in contrast to the Spirit-based worldview of the scriptures and spiritual faith.

The world that we see revealed by our senses as we look around is a world of surfaces. A world of things that can be compared, measured, weighed, balanced, analyzed and counted. This tangible realm is very seductive because it is so attractive since it presents itself to us with such potency. It is easy to forget to notice that the part that we see is riding on something else. If we look a little deeper, if we look behind the surfaces, we will understand that the word sin is referring to living as though God were not here, living as though God is not real, living as though God is absent, and living as though we are just our physical appearance.

We must remember that deeper than all the surface appearances is our essential being. The essential being of everything is invisible. It is a creation in the mind of God, and we human beings are creations in the mind of God. We are far more than what appears between our hat and boots. There is a lot more to us than what we can see and compare, count and judge.

So sin is a way of living in relation to appearances only. Sin is living in separation. The Greek word itself, "*hamartia*" refers to missing the mark, like an archer would miss a target.

The whole mark of human life is the realization that the divine and human have come together in a dance of co-creativity, in which the will of God manifests us, offering us a will like unto God's so that we can choose to give ourselves back to God and know ourselves as a continuing physical, human manifestation and spiritual divinity at exactly the same time.

Sin lives on the surface. It keeps us living in separation, alienated from the essence of Spirit and from each other. Sin generates a feeling of cut-off-ness and separation. It fosters a kind of doubt-filled anxiety that keeps us feeling threatened, cautious and un-free.

As an analogy, imagine that there is a great sphere of being. If you look around at the cosmos, you might conclude that God loves spheres. God loves solar spheres and earthly spheres and lunar spheres. There is a great sphere of being in which God is the very center that emanates the Whole. All appearances ride over the surface of this sphere.

If you look at only surfaces then you cannot see God. Living on the surface, as though the surface is all there is – is the life of sin and separation. It is a life of alienation in which we live in constant anxiety and fear, afraid that we will not be able to protect ourselves against other appearances. We forget that our life is not in the appearance. Our life is in the invisible manifesting presence that animates the appearances and gives it meaning.

The essence of things is qualitative. They cannot be analyzed and compared, counted, weighed or balanced. The supreme quality of everything is the love that manifests and maintains the whole creation, holding it together in a single, indivisible unity.

In that love, appearances can come together in the divine dance. In that love, we do not have to protect our self against each other. We learn to bear each other. We love each other and serve each other, participating in this co-creation with each other. We no longer have to live in comparisons that leave us feeling dead inside. Thus the call of the Lenten journey, and indeed of the entire Christian journey, is a call to come back to the spherical center,

just underneath the appearances of all things, including
ourselves.

We heard from the prophet Joel, "Return to your heart."
We heard the call of the 51st Psalm, "Create in me a clean
heart, O Lord." We heard Paul talking about the heart.
And we heard Jesus saying, do not do things for the sake
of appearances where they are counted or measured, but
do things for the Spirit.

We meet the Spirit in our hearts. Sin is the realm of the
head, the realm that divides things up, separates them,
counts them, compares them, and judges them as right
and wrong. It is perpetually recreating Adam's sin of judging good from evil.

When we understand the One presence and power that is
divine love, creating and maintaining the wholeness of all
things, then we will realize it is infinitely and essentially
good. Remember, the creation allegory in Genesis announces that God goes through a series of steps to manifest this world, ultimately calling the creation good at
every stage. But when God came to human beings, God
said, these are "*very* good."

So what is the fall? It is the fall upward into our heads,
and into the head's values. It is the fall into thinking to
the exclusion of the values of the heart where the qualities of Life live. In the heart we will see beauty, experience
joy and feel a peace that surpasses understanding. Can we
feel the love that makes us see other human beings, not
as objects to be competed with or to get something from,
but as manifestations of God to be savored and delighted
in? Will we experience the joy of seeing past the appear-

ances and into the essence of our own being and the being of others?

We are constantly seduced between attention to physical facts revealed by our senses, and the remembering of the spirit in our hearts. It is the heart that is the essence of our Life. It is where our Life lives. A cerebral intellectuality that knows everything by its name is a seduction that leaves us in sin.

Remember Adam was given the power by God at the very beginning of humanity to name and count things in the creation. But if we do so without God we have lost the essential meaning of our roles as stewards of the creation. We have slipped into that state of consciousness called sin. We become Adam, that is, the primal human all over again.

Without going into theological detail, Paul has told us that the purpose of Christ was to get us out of this mess. We could not figure our own way out of it. The complexities of the webs of judgment and intrigue that have woven us into the fabric of our lives are so pervasive and mean-spirited that when you see them it is appalling. One begins to realize that we could not get ourselves out of this mess on our own.

So what are we going to do? We are going to give ourselves back to Christ. Christ is the Way. Christ reveals the way, not to our heads but to our hearts. Christ allows us, for some mysterious purpose, to come out of this mess of judgment and back into the love that God is.

Now Christ tells us, and warns us along the way, that the return journey to the sphere of God is filled with pitfalls, that the journey back to the heart from the head, is filled with seductions. We will be tempted to adopt the values of the head and to put religious clothes on them, to dress them up in spiritual finery so that they still keep the head's agenda foremost in our minds and do not allow us the return journey to the heart.

Thus the seduction of a time like Lent, when we are adopting some spiritual practices, is to do them for the sake of doing them – to be seen by others – but not only by others, but also parts of the head that say, "O look at me; I am fasting from television. Wow, that is pretty spiritual. I am not going to read the news for an entire 40 days. Wow, am I doing God a favor. O, my goodness, God probably loves me now!" This inner commentary has nothing to do with the heart. This has nothing to do with inner qualities of Spirit. This has nothing to do with the deeply felt joy of simply being. It certainly will not lead us to the peace that passes understanding.

If we want a clean heart, then we will have to attend to the values of the heart. We will need to learn to give our attention to the things that are a little deeper than the surfaces, and a little deeper than the surfaces of ourselves. What this means is almost radically unbelievable.

Are you ready to hear something that is really challenging? Forget about your own behavior. Forget about what you are doing. Forget about comparing your behavior to prior behavior, or anticipating better behavior in the future as you engage on this path of improvement. There is no improvement; you do not need to improve.

The path of Christian grace is the path of God's love, a love that embraces even our human imperfections. His love is so perfect, so whole, so complete and so all-embracing that He does not even notice our imperfections or misbehavior. When we abide in our own hearts, living in secret from our own actions, not even paying attention to our own actions or the actions of others, a new world of love opens up to us. We begin to see with new eyes, to hear with new ears, and to live from a new heart – a place we scarcely suspected was even there. From the perspective of the head-bound world, this way of life makes no sense. Sometimes it seems the head's sole agenda is judging sense-based behavior. From the perspective of the heart, love trumps all things and sets us free to truly live.

Behaviors are of no interest to God; behaviors are of tremendous importance to us. But the attention to behaviors, whether better ones or worse ones, is what leaves us living on the surfaces of things. Meanwhile, in the heart, the love of God is ever present.

God is not transcendently somewhere else. God is not a God who created in the past and is not here now. God is always in the present tense. God is the one who breaths us, and beats our hearts and brings light to our minds. God is the present tense in every way.

Why do we not notice it? One reason might be because we are monitoring behaviors – ours and others. We are judging with critical attention that which should be and should not be. The very fact that something just *is*, acknowledges that good must be in it somewhere or it could not have crossed the threshold from non-being into being.

So to live in constant relation to the good means that we have to give up this attention to the senses and the objects they reveal, and come into the sweet presence of the heart and abide there for no reason at all except that it is possible. When we get a taste for it we will not want to move our attention back into the judgment of our heads.

The third Chinese patriarch of Zen, in his amazing discourse on the mind of faith, refers to judging in a way that has had a profound impact on me for many years. He refers to it as the burdensome practice of judging. "If you wish to abide in truth", he says, "alive to the single way, then pay no attention to this or that and have no opinion about anything. If you wish to see the truth and abide in the single way then have no preferences."

Is it possible to have no preference? Nobody can answer that question for you. You have to answer that yourself. The price of admission, the price of finding the answer to that question is to drop into your heart. Close the door to the mind and all the burdensome practices of the judging self. Discover the answer by breathing into that space, and by listening. It is a return journey to a place as close as the heart. It only requires our attention.

Lent is a time of releasing ourselves from the burdensome practice of judging. It is a season of listening in the desert where the night air and the sounds of life are so clear and undisturbed that they become the gift you were looking for all along.

Sin is not an accusation. It is a description of a state of consciousness that is like living in the shadows. It is like living in a mockery of reality. The heart is where our Life is. This is where the truth is and Christ is our Way there.

Everything we are looking for is in the heart. Close the door; give up the senses for a minute and all the prior conditioning from them. Pray to your Father in secret, and your Father who sees will reward you (Matthew 6.6). That is a promise. God does not make promises that God cannot and will not deliver on. Yet, there are all types of people who do not believe, and therefore miss the mark completely. Amen.[12]

∞

Thirteen

Maundy Thursday

and

Good Friday

∞

"Jesus knew that his hour had come to depart from this world and go to the Father. Having loved his own who were in the world, he loved them to the end." John 13.1

Well we are all here courtesy of Judas Iscariot. We owe him big time. On Good Friday we appreciate what Grace has brought us. We appreciate the gift of transformation. If we understand that these gifts are through the passion, death, resurrection and ascension of Jesus then we have to realize that the entire process was perfect, and required every person in the drama to play their part perfectly, including Judas.

The narrative of a God who dies and is resurrected is found in Babylonian, Egyptian and countless other historic cultures. The whole drama of the death and resurrection of a seed is also the story of nature every spring. But the point of the historical events of Maundy Thursday and Good Friday is that the drama had to be played out not just in the ephemeral realms of human imagination, but also on the stage of history. The reality needed to become efficacious and available for humankind, and as such, it had to be played out on the stage of history, with real names, real suffering and real blood.

Now we may not understand the mechanics of all this, but the truth of the matter is that we are here because it happened in history. Every person played a part, and Judas played his well. He paid a very high price for it, and we are beholden to him in some deep, mysterious way. Amen.[13]

∞

Fourteen

Easter

∞

"If there is no resurrection of the dead, then Christ has not been raised; and if Christ has not been raised, then our proclamation has been in vain and your faith has been in vain." 1 Corinthians 15.13-14

Today is the most challenging day of the Christian liturgical year. What happened, and why is it of interest to us? Can we really believe that there was a resurrection of a dead body and the disappearance of a corpse?

Now there are ways to accept this as a belief. But there are also ways to understand and experience it. When we understand the great events that took place two thousand years ago, and relate them to our lives now, we can begin to participate in an event that is continuously happening, instead of thinking of the resurrection as *just* an important event to believe in.

Hopefully today we become not just believers, but experiencers of the risen Presence, and participants in the ongoing incarnation, the continuous incarnation of Christ in this world. Hopefully on Easter Sunday we will become a people who choose to live in the new creation, living in a brand new world, in a brand new way, because we have been fundamentally changed in the same way the apostles and disciples were changed two thousand years ago.

Mysterious? Yes. Just as mysterious as the Eucharist is. But relatable? You bet it is. When we come into relationship with the truth of the resurrected Christ, such mysteries become self-evident to us. Though we cannot explain them with our rational minds, though they do not add up rationally, they become such a personal experience that you would not even think to question them.

Today we celebrate Christ's resurrection. Today we realize that there is more to us than the average consciousness we walk around in every day. When we are lifted up in this way we become elevated in spirit. Why does it take a special moment for this to happen? Why cannot we be elevated in spirit all the time? We can be, yet the point is to learn and educate ourselves in how to experience it. We learn how to be receptive to this risen Presence, which so many people have received and then said to themselves, "O my God! I get it now."

The process of the resurrected Christ appearing to us happens in stages. It happens first with a Presence that is scarcely recognizable, then with a Presence that is recognizable. After which is often the attempt to grab and hold onto it. Finally, there is the vanishing and ascension. Remember Jesus said to Mary: "You cannot grab me, you cannot touch me, do not cling to me." One of the difficulties about Easter is that we want to objectify Jesus. We want to be able to hold onto Him for the reassurance we so desperately seek in a world that seems to have no safety in it. But in this vanishing and ascension, Christ reappears to us internally in the risen state, invisible to our sense-bound eyes, but completely and utterly visible to the eyes of faith and to the experience of our burning hearts.

We are culturally inclined to think about things. Though our heads are useful tools, and though they have given us technological capacities that are astounding, the fact remains that the seat of the soul, the seat of truth, and the place of the Presence is in our hearts. When our hearts "burn," we know we are in touch with the truth. Not when we get satisfying intellectual explanations, not when we feel we are in the right with the correct beliefs that are set over and against other people who do not know. Christ came to abolish all the divisions.

In Paul we have a very clear statement of this reality: "In Christ there is neither Jew nor Greek, nor slave or free" (Galatians 3.28). We might as well extend that to all of the opposites of this world; no more divisions. Christ is one. Divine Presence is one. Divine love is one. Divine life is one and Christ is known in this unity from the heart. The heart sees with single-eyed vision. It sees and experiences the oneness everywhere, ever able to appreciate the heart in another.

Differences, the making important of differences, the judging by appearances, the making of "other" – these are all the fingerprints of the head. The head is what has brought us to this state of fragmented confusion where we are alienated from our earth, alienated from our Source, alienated from others who do not look like us or believe like us or act like us.

No state of mind could be further from what the risen Christ is offering us. When our eyes are single, when our eyes are one, it is the eye of the heart that is operative. The heart sees God everywhere and in everything. It blesses and experiences God in every human being and in every creature. Our work then is to in some way return to the Garden of Eden, which is in our hearts. It is a paradox of unity and Presence with God. The resurrection of Christ plays a big part in our freedom to now return to our second innocence.

How do we do that? We do it through daily practice. We already practice being in the head virtually 24 hours a day with news programs and all the ways our cultural gossip separates us and makes people seem like "other." For a few minutes each day, we can settle into the vast silence from which we are constantly emerging and to which we will all return, the Source of every form that ever came and the end of every form that will ever come. We find in our hearts a vast silence, indeed, the touch of eternal Life – an eternal Life that the head does not know what to do with.

There is no way we can experience this at a distance. It is not a spectator sport. By a daily practice, by living within a conceptual Christian framework and descending into our hearts, we experience a new creation. This is not something that will happen in the future; it has already happened and is already here. If we are waiting for something in the world to change, well, it is not going to do that. The change we are waiting for is in ourselves, in our own hearts.

We are the new creation. The call to participate is the call to each one of us to get real. This is not "get real," as in a funny way, but become Real with a capital "R." Enter into that which never changes, which is always here, which is always the same for every person in every situation and in every time and for every culture. The eternal Presence of God is waiting for each of us in our hearts, and Christ has shown us the way.

We look for easy and quick answers like scientists who want to get to the bottom line. But when a person spends an entire life pondering the mystery, seeking out meanings, looking into the scriptures and looking into the heart, then we have a model to approach the contemplative life. It is not filled with rational answers. It is filled with relationship, with a continuous unfolding of the touch and Presence of God that leads us ever deeper into the direct experience of Christ's risen presence.

God is the only Reality. It is right now, in Christ that we live and move and have our being. It is God who breathes us, who is beating our hearts. To make that unreal, and to live as though we were at risk, as though other people were objects, this is what sin is. It is the unreality of God. It is making the unreal, which is our world of thoughts and conditions, as though it were real. When we make God unreal, we treat God as if God were somewhere else, some other place we hope to go some day. Meanwhile we are missing God right now, and this is what "sin" means. That is to say, God is the mark we are missing.

The scriptures call us to love God with all our heart and soul and mind and strength. That would mean loving the God who is here and now. If we are not doing that, we are living in sin. We are living fallen from reality. It does not mean we are bad people, it just means that we have forgotten who we are. It also probably means we are living in a cultural mindset that has no relationship to reality.

So what are we? Are we just bodies and death? Identities and life? We sometimes say, when we skin a knee, "I hurt myself." Are these bodies that we see the sum and substance of our lives? True, the body has *bios*, that is, biological life. It shares that life with all animals, and it shares with all animals the disappearance of that body too. The body is going to go away. If we are going to identify with "myself" as being this body, it is no wonder we fear "going away" because we have watched and seen all the people of history disappear. The body of those we have loved is not among us anymore. But is the body the extent of human identity? No, not at all.

What Christ would have us know is that *bios* is not the only life. There is another kind of life, and it is Life itself. It is a Life that does not come and go. A Life that does not start and stop. A Life that does not have a beginning and an ending as the physical appearance of the body has. It is this Life, the Life of Christ, in which our true identity is. Rather than imagine the physical body re-enlivened exactly as it was before, we have to take the clues from the apostles, from those who met Jesus in his resurrected form that he was still with them in some form of bodily presence but not the same form as they had known before.

The deep mystery of resurrection is that we have another body. Christ's presence is the eternal Life within us, that Christ is now and always our true identity. Christ liberates us from death by liberating us from the idea that we are just the physical body we see in the mirror, helping us to understand the ineffable mystery that we are as Christ is – participants in vast, infinite Life.

The human being is a most mysterious creation. In many ways we are like animals. We share with animals the physical appearance and biological qualities of the senses. But far more than animals, we are the creatures who can ponder, marvel and reflect at our own existence. We are the creatures who can have the x-ray eyes of faith that allow us to see into the spiritual world, beyond the worlds of form and into eternal Life where our true identity – is always alive, now and forever – waiting for us to discover.

What is the price of this discovery? Everything the culture models to us. Ours is a culture of death. We often live constrained by fear, holding on so tightly to the life we think we have that we are missing the Life we already *are*. The radiant, eternal, absolutely loving Presence is waiting for us to discover its presence within.

For example, when Jesus was talking to his disciples in the farewell discourses in the Gospel of John, he said, "Listen, I have got to go. Where I am going you cannot follow right now, but if I do not go, you will never be able to get there" (John 14-17). It is normal to want to hold on to Jesus in his literal, physical form. But why? Perhaps we want an object because we think we are objects. Jesus understands our human predicament and says, "If I do not disappear as an object, you will never stop searching for me that way." Likewise, if we do not let go of ourselves as objects, we will never discover ourselves as participants of the eternal *I am*.

Through Christ's resurrection we can begin to understand and experience that we bear the family name "I am." We all know it intuitively. We are *being* itself. *Being* alive. The call of Easter is to participate in the resurrection, to take these lives and live them out to the fullest in their ordinary extraordinariness. We can fearlessly live our lives with God on the stage of history, not reserving them or holding them back, but living fully the values of the beatitudes. In this way, there is nothing to fear. When we know ourselves in Christ as Truth and Life, we have discovered the way to God that Jesus spoke of (John 14.6). It is here. It is now, and it is always waiting to be discovered. Through the resurrection, death has no more significance for us because we know that it simply means, not a loss of our lives, but a return to the Father.

"Fear not little flock," Jesus said, "It is your Father's good pleasure to give you the kingdom." When we give up making ourselves little gods, and our disdain for the multiple ways in which God has made human beings to appear, and when we let go of our script for how Christ ought to be and how life ought to be, we discover Life as our lives. We discover the infinite and eternal Presence that is uncaused joy. It is the peace that passes understanding. It needs no explanation.

The reason Christianity is here today is not because people believed it. It is because the first-century Christians did not have any explanation for it. They were experiencing it. They were different than they were before they experienced Christ's risen Presence within them. The joy they felt at the overcoming of fear was a joy so great that it was like a positive infection of light. It communicated itself like a living fire all around the Mediterranean basin.

Then Christianity had the great misfortune, perhaps, to be made the politically correct religion of the Roman Empire. With the Edict of Milan in 313 C.E., it became increasingly fashionable to be a Christian. It became something one could believe in and be known by and was seen as a club one could join. Fortunately, despite this cultural form of Christianity, the same Real call to Life is still here. Generations of people have experienced it for themselves and continue to feel and know beyond knowing that their life is hidden with Christ in God.

He is risen. He is here now. We find Christ by the Spirit within. He changed my life, not because I believed something, but by experiencing and loving Christ I finally experienced my life as the Christ-Life too. He is within us now. We shall walk His way and we shall never die. Amen.[14]

∞

Part Three:

Contemplative

Prayers to Abba

∞

Fifteen

Prayers for Remembering

∞

"Contemplative prayer is the world in which God can do anything. To move into that realm is the greatest adventure."

- Thomas Keating, *Open Mind, Open Heart*

Prayer at the Beginning of Worship

Most gracious and merciful God, our Father and our Mother, our Life: What an amazing realization it is to recognize that you have brought us here and put your living Word before us and given us an opportunity to come face to face with Reality. Lord, open our minds and our hearts beyond their usual slumber. Open us Lord to the radiant reality that you are. Let your Holy Spirit move in each of us to bring us to some personal understanding and realization of Truth through our encounter with your Word. Move in each and every one of us in an obvious and unmistakable way to make it absolutely clear and unavoidably evident that you are our God, and that we are your people and that you always hear and answer our prayers. We pray this in the name of the Father and of the Son and in the name of the Holy Spirit.

Offering Invitation and Prayer

There is plenty of relief to be had by just remembering. One of the areas we can remember is with our supply. We always feel lack around supply and so when we are in a moment of gathered attention it is good to take our tithes and offerings in our hands and recognize where they come from and how we have always been supplied even in the midst of all our doubts: So we bless our tithes and offerings with our knowledge of what has always been true – that God's love has always met and will always meet all my needs. I give freely and receive joyfully. Let us know the truth together: God's love has always met and will always meet all my needs. I give freely and receive joyfully. And how blessed we are when we simply re-member God. Amen.

Breathing now the air of Spirit, we dedicate these tithes and offerings to the victory of consciously chosen love in each of our lives and on our planet, over the lie that we are separate, and our useless acting out from fear. In Christ we pray. Amen.

Prayer before the Eucharist

Lord Jesus, living and eternal Christ, we feel your risen presence as the very Life that pervades and yet transcends our bodies and our minds. We realize you are the way and the truth, and are grateful to share in your body and your blood. May our participation in these divine mysteries transform us into one, in your mystical body, the true body of Christ for the glory of God our Father, for the glory of His kingdom here on earth so that our joy might be complete. We pray this in your most holy and precious name. Amen.

Prayer for Oneness

Lord God of all creation, almighty and merciful Father, what a blessing it is to realize it is you who has called us together. It is you who holds us together in your love while we grow, and you who feed our spirits with your living Word. Lord, help each one of us to come open-minded and open-hearted, to have a face-to-face and personal encounter with your Word. Let our understanding be transformative. Let the spiritual food that you have for us lift us from the feeling of separation and isolation into the unity of your Holy Spirit. Move in us, Lord, in clear and obvious ways to make it unmistakable that this is your church, that we are your people, and that you are the living and eternal God who always hears and answers our every prayer. We pray this in the name of the Father and of the Son and of the Holy Spirit. Amen.

Prayer for Future Blessings

Most gracious and merciful God, our Mother and our Father, our creator, sustainer, leader and teacher, what a grace it is to realize you, and to realize that you have been living our lives, and that you have been guiding all our steps, that you have called us deeper and deeper into your great heart of love, and that you have gathered us so that each of us might come face to face with your living Word. Lord help us to become open-minded and open-hearted, to meet your Word in a way that leaves us open to see and be healed by it. To be enriched and filled by it. Thank you for this opportunity, Lord. Thank you for all the beings who have walked this way before us, whose efforts have made it possible for us to be here today. May the efforts that we make to receive and bear the teaching be worthy of the ones who have gone on before us. And may the results of our efforts be a blessing to those who have yet to come. Move in us in an obvious way, Lord. We pray this in the name of the Father and of the Son and of the Holy Spirit. Amen

Prayer at Mealtime

Abba, thank you for calling us together and that through the touch of our hands in this circle we feel our oneness. Bless all who have brought us this food today, from the farmer and trucker to those who have prepared it. Make it useful for our transformation in Christ for your glory. May those who are hungry at this hour somehow feel the touch of your love and may we recognize the presence of Christ in those we serve today through the strength we gain from this meal. Amen.

∞

Conclusion:

Let's leave that right there

∞

Tim occasionally concludes his sermons with the simple saying, "I think we will leave that right there." It is a gracious way of gently cooling off the preaching-jets after a transmission has occurred. In truth, if time were not a factor, one gets the sense that Tim could continue transmitting indefinitely.

No matter the length of the teaching, open-hearted listeners are the beneficiaries of Tim's overflowing and accumulated understanding, which he, in humility and love, wishes to share with his friends. It is understanding that Tim conveys through his presence, and this understanding is bearing the fruit of God-devotion in community. There is a Work saying that "the teacher is the elder in understanding," and that "understanding is the union of knowledge and being."

It is that particular touch of friendship imbued with understanding that verifies the presence of Christian love and humility in Tim's preaching, so beautifully captured by St. Paul in his summation of the Incarnation of Jesus the Christ, and his apostolic invitation for us to follow:

> "Let each of you look not to your own interests, but to the interests of others. Let the same mind be in you that was in

Christ Jesus, who, though he was in the form of God, did not regard equality with God...but emptied himself, taking the form of a servant...he humbled himself and became obedient to the point of death – even death on a cross" (Philippians 2.4-8).

My dear reader, may these sermons stimulate deeper transformation into the mind of Christ, which is the fullness of understanding possible for us. May they sustain us with grace so to bear with one another through future difficulties, and may they reveal to us the hidden benefits of dying to self while living toward God, in whose love we are eternally held, healed, helped and graciously drawn forward in growth.

Glory be to God,
our Source and Sustainer,
now and always.
Amen.

∞

Further Resources

∞

For diverse and useful resources for your ongoing growth on the spiritual journey, please visit:

www.ConsciousHarmony.org

www.ContemplativeOutreach.org

Further Reading

∞

The following bibliography is a sampling of books that have informed and shaped Tim's teaching:

Lectio Divina

Nan C. Merrill, *Psalms for Praying: An Invitation to Wholeness*

M. Basil Pennington, *Lectio Divina: Renewing the Ancient Practice of Praying the Scriptures*

Centering Prayer

Carl Arico, *A Taste for Silence*

Thomas Keating, *Open Mind, Open Heart*

The Work

Maurice Nicoll, *Psychological Commentaries on the Teaching of Gurdjieff and Ouspensky, Vol. 1 – 6*

----------- *Living Time and the Integration of the Life*

Esoteric Christianity

Robin Amis, *A Different Christianity*

Anonymous, *Meditations on the Tarot: A Journey into Christian Hermeticisim*

Boris Mouravieff, *Gnosis, Vol. 1 – 3*

Contemplative Christianity

Thomas Keating, *Contemplative Christianity*

---------- *The Mystery of Christ*

Bernadette Roberts, *The Experience of No Self*

----------*What Is Self?*

Theology

James Alison, *The Joy of Being Wrong*

Gil Bailie, *Violence Unveiled: Humanity at the Crossroads*

Llia Delio, *Christ in Evolution*

Sebastian Moore, *The Crucified Jesus Is No Stranger*

Raimon Panikkar, *Christophany: The Fullness of Man*

About Tim Cook

∞

© Deborah Cannon The STATESMAN

Tim Cook is the Minister of The Church of Conscious Harmony in Austin, Texas with wife Barbara as co-minister. Tim was ordained in 1983 by the Unity School of Christianity and is a former pastor of Unity Church of Austin. He has been a regional coordinator for Contemplative Outreach and acknowledges two decades of influence from Father Thomas Keating. Tim and Barbara's intention in the establishment of The Church of Conscious Harmony is to build a community of people who want to make God-devotion the center of their lives while living in the ordinary world without the aid of monastery walls.

"The whole point lies in how you recover from falling, and it is always interesting to notice how people recover from a bad [inner] state because here lays the Work at first – in this learning to walk instead of always falling, because we are like little children learning to walk and if we never fell we could never learn."

- *Maurice Nicoll, Psychological Commentaries, Page 645*

"I have said these things to you while I am still with you. But the Advocate, the Holy Spirit, whom the Father will send in my name, will you teach you everything, and remind you of all that I have said to you."

- *John 14.25*

Notes

∞

All sermons were preached by Rev. Tim Cook and recorded in the Sanctuary at The Church of Conscious Harmony, Austin, Texas. The sermons are available for purchase as CD's from the church bookstore.

Please visit www.ConsciousHarmony.org for further information.

∞

[1] Tim Cook, Sermon, Sunday, November 15, 2010. Liturgical readings: *1 Samuel 1.4-20; Hebrews 10.11-25; Mark 13.1-8.*

[2] Tim Cook, Sermon, Sunday, June 27, 2010. Liturgical readings: *1 Kings 19.16-21; Psalm 16.1-11; Galatians 5.1, 13-18.*

[3] Tim Cook, Sermon, Wednesday, November 24, 2010. Liturgical readings: *Revelation 15.1-4; Psalm 98.1-9; Luke 21.12-19.*

[4] Tim Cook, Sermon, Wednesday, June 3, 2009. Liturgical readings: *Psalm 25; Mark 12.18-37.*

[5] Tim Cook, Sermon, Wednesday, May 20, 2009. Liturgical readings: *Acts 17; Psalm 148; John 16.12-15.*

[6] Tim Cook, Sermon, Wednesday, July 22, 2009. Liturgical readings: *Song of Songs 3.1-4; Psalm 78; John 20.1-18.*

[7] Tim Cook, Sermon, Wednesday, November 17, 2010. Liturgical readings: *Revelation 4.1-11; Psalm 150; Luke 19.11-28.*

[8] Tim Cook, Sermon, Sunday, December 6, 2009. Liturgical readings: *Psalm 126; Philippians 1.4-11; Luke 3.1-6.*

[9] Tim Cook, Sermon, Wednesday, December 23, 2009. Liturgical reading: *Luke 1.57-66.*

[10] Tim Cook, Sermon, Thursday, December 24, 2009. Liturgical readings: *Luke 2; John 1.*

[11] Tim Cook, Sermon, Wednesday, February 12, 2010. Liturgical readings: *Jonah 3.1-10; Psalm 51; Luke 11.29-32.*

[12] Tim Cook, Sermon, Wednesday, February 17, 2010. Liturgical readings: *Joel 2.12-18; Psalm 51; Matthew 6.1-18.*

[13] Tim Cook, Sermon, Thursday, April 9, 2009. Liturgical reading: *John 13.1-15.*

[14] Tim Cook, Sermon, Sunday, April 4, 2010. Liturgical readings: *John 20.1-23; 1 Corinthians 15.*

9076644R00102

Made in the USA
San Bernardino, CA
04 March 2014